one man's real-life journey
from unspeakable memories
to unbelievable grace . . .

undaunted

Josh McDowell *with* Cristóbal Krusen

TYNDALE™
MOMENTUM

An Imprint of
Tyndale House Publishers, Inc.

TYNDALE is a registered trademark of Tyndale House Publishers, Inc. *Tyndale Momentum* and the Tyndale Momentum logo are trademarks of Tyndale House Publishers, Inc. Tyndale Momentum is an imprint of Tyndale House Publishers, Inc.

Undaunted: One Man's Real-Life Journey from Unspeakable Memories to Unbelievable Grace

Designed by Daniel Farrell

Edited by Bonne Steffen

Undaunted is a true story. Many of the names have been changed to protect the privacy of individuals or their families. Although the events actually happened, some characters are composites of various people in the author's life.

ISBN 978-1-62090-883-9

Printed in the United States of America

I affectionately dedicate this book to my four beloved children—Kelly, Sean, Katie, and Heather—and to their lifelong mates: Michael, Stephanie, Jerry, and David. I also dedicate these pages of memories to my precious grandchildren: Scottie, Shauna, Quinn, Beckett, and Brenna, as well as to all those who will come after them (we eagerly await your arrival!).

I pray that my life story will inspire each one of you to trust our Lord, no matter what circumstances you face. May you always remember and defend Romans 1:16.

Contents

Preface

MANY PEOPLE are familiar with aspects of my early life. Over the years, I have shared some of the details in various formats, mostly in my presentations. But it hasn't been until now that I have pulled back the curtain to give a fuller picture.

For many years, I have been approached by groups and individuals to make a movie about my early life and testimony. I never felt comfortable doing that until I met award-winning filmmaker Cristóbal Krusen five years ago. I entrusted to him the challenge of bringing my story to life.

That's what this book is at heart. It's a story—my story, painted in broad strokes to trace the highs and lows of my early life experience. The events are true, though some of the people you'll meet are composites of several people in my life; most of the conversations within the scenes are recollected to the best of my knowledge. It's called *Undaunted* because it sums up in one word who I was, whether I knew it at the time or not. I faced severe challenges growing up, and my instinctive reaction was to give as good as I got. I ascribed to Nietzsche's philosophy "What does not kill me makes me stronger," without any inkling of who he was.

Adversity did make me strong and determined. But it was a superficial strength, a defense mechanism, an artificial mask that hid dark things. What I longed for—what we all long for—was a loving relationship with someone who accepted me for who I was, no matter what.

By the time I was eleven years old, I considered myself the loneliest, most God-forsaken person on the planet. For reasons you will read about, I abandoned the notion that a family provides stability, that a father provides protection, that others can be trusted. I turned my back on God as well; the only names I called Him were flung at Him in angry, vile curses. I was not about to admit my shortcomings or weaknesses. Unfortunately, I did not understand how destructive it is to one's soul to live in denial of the truth.

I fought to make sure my deep fears and insecurities about things that had happened to me would remain secrets. I was the emotional equivalent of the clever illiterate who manages to convince others he knows how to read and write.

There may be aspects of my story that you will recognize in your own life story, while other things—thankfully—are only mine to tell. And even with the pain I have gone through, I am certain that millions of people have had a rougher, more difficult upbringing than I experienced.

The fact is that no one goes through life unscathed.

The biblical book of Job says that "people are born for trouble as readily as sparks fly up from a fire." I had a lot of sparks in my life, including one life-changing spark that brought me hope. I invite you to read and consider how—with the help of One stronger than yourself—you, too, can face life undaunted.

Josh McDowell
APRIL 2012

1

All's Right with the World

IT WAS AN UNUSUALLY warm day for so early in spring, and my car windows were rolled down to catch whatever breeze there might be in Wheaton, Illinois, thirty miles west of Chicago. I was a junior at Wheaton College, working my afternoon job of delivering administrative papers to local high schools. More than a part-time job, it provided me a small break from the unrelenting pressures of the academic workload at college.

I had hoped to get across the tracks at the Chase Street crossing before the Chicago commuter train rumbled past, but it seemed my approach was choreographed to coincide precisely with the lowering of the gate and the flashing of the red warning lights. I pulled to a stop and leaned back in my seat to relax. The clanging of the signal played a discordant counterrhythm to the number one hit song the Shirelles were singing on the car radio—"Will You Still Love Me Tomorrow?"

I glanced in my rearview mirror at the serene view of the Wheaton campus extending up the hill behind me, with venerable Blanchard Hall at its apex. The scene brought to mind the words of Jesus in the Gospel of Matthew: "A city that is set on a hill cannot be hidden."

Would I leave a mark on the world for Wheaton? If so, what would it be?

My eyes turned back to the passing train. Such a soothing sound it made. I remembered lying in bed at night as a child, listening to the freight trains that passed by, their sound rolling unimpeded over the Michigan farmland. How resolute the locomotives seemed to be, their horns blaring fearlessly in the dark while the boxcars clattered rhythmically behind, their sound rocking me to sleep.

I sighed contentedly. For some reason, I thought of Robert Browning's oft-quoted line, "God's in His heaven, all's right with the world."

I sang along with the car radio,

So tell me now, and I won't ask again,
Will you still love me tomorrow?

Suddenly, in the rearview mirror, I noticed a pickup truck barreling toward me, swerving erratically and gathering speed instead of slowing down. I blinked hard and looked again. The vehicle was not going to stop—it had no time or room to stop. With the train still passing in front of me, I reached for the gear shift to put the car in reverse, but there was no time to back out of the way. The truck was nearly on top of me when I threw the gear into neutral, pressed down on the brake as hard as I could, and braced for impact.

In a split second, my life flashed before me—a life that, for the most part, I wanted to forget.

2

In the Beginning

THERE'S A SAYING that childhood is the most beautiful of life's seasons. And so it should be. But that was not true in my case. Though it pains me to say it, I believe the main reason my father wanted me born was to have an extra worker on the farm. He said as much on numerous occasions as I was growing up. I did have the unfettered run (often barefoot) of our family farm in Union City, Michigan, and found a measure of stability in my mother, my chores, and school, in that order. But the relationship with my dad proved difficult. How do you earn the love and respect of a man who treats you more as a hired hand than a son?

Wilmot McDowell was born in Indiana in 1898, one of ten children. At some point, he moved to Fremont County in Idaho, where he met and married my mother, Edith Joslin, in 1919. Their first child, Wilmot Jr., was born two years later.

Dad was not a big man physically, but he had a rough-and-tumble frontier spirit that served him well as a truck driver hauling produce and lumber through the Targhee Pass to the copper and silver mines of Montana. Anything could happen on those remote and isolated roads, and often did. Early on, Dad learned to extricate himself from difficult situations by whatever means necessary.

Mom, by contrast, was more refined. She had been born and raised in New Jersey and came primarily from English stock. She prided herself on being a cultured lady and maintaining proper etiquette around the house. What she saw in my dad, well . . . I can only surmise they fell in love and got married before he became an alcoholic.

During the 1920s, the economy took a downturn in Idaho, and after the birth of my sister Shirley, the family moved east, settling in Detroit. It wasn't long before Dad's drinking problem cost him his job at a big A&P store there, and the family moved again—this time to the Battle Creek area, 120 miles to the west. The Great Depression had begun.

During this difficult time for all Americans, a wealthy friend of the family I would later come to know as Aunt Liz gave Mom and Dad a piece of farmland on the outskirts of Union City. Her goal was to help my parents get a fresh start in life. But nothing started over, unless you count the birth of my second sister, June, in 1930.

Dad managed the local A&P store in Union City until his chronic drinking cost him that job as well. There was nothing left for him to do but try to make a go of dairy farming. The results weren't particularly auspicious. Fortunately for everyone in the family, Wilmot Jr. (or Junior as we called him) had begun to show an aptitude for farming at an early age and was already involved in managing the farm by the time Dad became unemployed. Junior joined the FFA (Future Farmers of America), and as a young teen he began to implement what he called a "scientific approach" to farming. Though he suffered from a congenital heart condition, he was a hard worker. Junior was very bright and did well in school. With Mom keeping the books, the farm was fairly profitable.

It didn't take long, however, for Dad to run things into the ground, thanks to his three-bottles-a-day wine habit and know-it-all attitude. There was a running battle between Junior and Dad. Junior resented Dad's interference in how he managed the farm, but despite their arguments, Junior was clearly Dad's favorite of all the children. Kind of gives you an idea how the rest of us got along with him.

Junior was eighteen years old when I was born, and Shirley a year younger than Junior. My sister June was ten.

The story goes that on one warm day in August 1939, the minister of the local Congregational church paid a visit to our house. We weren't a churchgoing family, but the minister was young and enthusiastic, new to his job. He had probably heard a few unsavory reports about our family from people in town and viewed us as sheep in need of a shepherd. While he sat sipping tea with Mom in the living room, he had no idea she was nine months pregnant. And with good reason. Standing barely five feet four inches tall, Mom had a thyroid condition that caused her weight to fluctuate between 340 and 360 pounds. It may sound funny, but it's true: she couldn't walk through a doorway without hitting both sides. I imagine I must have been very well hidden inside her ample midsection.

When I came along a week or so later, the minister was flabbergasted to learn that another boy had been welcomed to the McDowell family! Mom made up for his embarrassment, I suppose, by taking me to church to be christened. I was given her maiden surname—Joslin—as my first name, though from an early age I would be called simply Jos. Unless, of course, Mom was upset with me about something or other. Then I heard, "Joslin David McDowell!"

Two weeks after I was born, Nazi Germany invaded Poland, and France and England declared war on Hitler. Following the bombing at Pearl Harbor a little more than two years later, my sister Shirley volunteered to serve in the army as a nurse. She was the first of my siblings to make the break from our unhappy home life.

Some of my earliest childhood memories are of Shirley coming home on leave. She always brought me a gift of some sort—toy soldiers or little army tanks made of tin. I always thought she looked so sharp in her military uniform, and pretty, too!

When I was four or five years old, Shirley came home with a tall army ranger named Stan. One day, she pulled me aside and whispered conspiratorially, "I'm going to marry Stan and help you get away from here, Jos. Who knows? Maybe one day you can come and stay with us."

The day finally arrived to say good-bye to Shirley. I held on to her and cried. I didn't want her to go. I had seen the newsreels at the movie theater in Battle Creek, so I knew that where she was going was dangerous . . . even deadly. But watching Shirley head out with Stan, you would have thought they were going to Florida or California on a carefree vacation.

Even when her tour of duty ended and she had the opportunity to leave the service and return home, she chose to stay on the front lines in Europe. I remember finding Mom crying in her bedroom one day, and I asked her what was wrong. I thought it was something Dad had done. But it wasn't. She had gotten a letter from Shirley, saying she was going to serve in Europe until the war was over.

Thankfully, Shirley survived the war. But she never came back home again to live. And for whatever reason, I never went to live with her and Stan when they got married and moved to Chicago, though I did visit sometimes.

The earliest of all my memories is my other sister, June, bathing me in the big concrete laundry tub on the enclosed porch. Because Mom was so overweight and couldn't get around easily, June would often spend time babysitting me. I remember taking trips into town with her when I was four and five years old. June was mature for her age and people often thought I was her son.

"What a cute little boy you have there," I remember an older woman saying to June on one such trip. She had stopped us on the sidewalk in Battle Creek and given me a little squeeze on the cheek. "Look at those merry blue eyes!" she said with a chuckle. "I bet he's into mischief now, ain't he?"

June smiled, playing along. "Oh, he's not such a bad boy. He does everything I tell him. Don't you, Jos?"

I nodded enthusiastically. "When I obey Mom, she always buys me ice cream!"

The stranger made more happy clucking noises and retrieved a quarter from her purse. "Well, let me buy you an ice cream, too, young man!" she exclaimed. Continuing on her way, she added aloud to herself: "Cute as a bug's ear!" June took me across the street to Sullivan's ice cream shop for a double vanilla cone.

I loved June. She was the sensitive, artistic one in the family and played the piano beautifully. She had what you might call an "old soul." I wonder what would have become of her if she hadn't married Merle Lowry—a man very much like Dad.

Merle didn't physically mistreat June (at least not much), but he was an alcoholic just the same. Unlike my father, he was outgoing. He would take me places and play catch with me in the yeard. He was a good refrigeration mechanic and was able to fix most anything, but his heavy drinking always held him back. It seemed he could never get his life together. I suppose June married him to get off the farm like Shirley had, and not too many years later she had five children. Six, if you included Merle.

I remember one Christmas, sitting around the tree waiting to open gifts, when my dad staggered in drunk. He collapsed on his chair and went to sleep while we waited for Merle to show up. But Merle never made it. We found out later he had careened off the road into a snowbank, and since he was too drunk to do anything about it, he just stayed there. He showed up the next morning to get drunk with Dad.

Not long after the war ended, Junior got hitched to a local gal named Carla, who was still a teenager at the time. No one in my family cared much for her—me included. Mom complained about Carla all the time.

Carla and Junior lived in a smaller house on the family property. I would often hear Carla reprimanding my brother for one thing or another because her voice carried a long distance. One day, Junior was cutting the grass in front of their house and accidentally ran over Carla's flower beds. You would have thought World War III had started the way she went after Junior, lashing out with her fists and her tongue.

Whenever Carla and Junior came over to the main house, she tried to order me around too. I remember the two of us getting into a fight because I wanted to listen to *The Green Hornet* on the radio and she wanted to listen to

The Burns and Allen Show. She changed the station twice and warned me to sit down and shut up. I promptly called her one of the names I'd heard Dad call Mom, and Carla chased me out of the house with threats of a "good hidin'." I climbed high up in the big willow tree next to the house, my safe refuge on numerous occasions. No one could get at me there. From that vantage point, I could shoot Carla with my slingshot if she came looking for me and be safely out of reach when I called her nasty names.

Sometimes it would be well past bedtime when I'd climb down the willow tree and sneak into the house through my bedroom window. I was banking on the probability that tomorrow would bring enough trouble of its own to get me off the hook. And it usually did.

Rounding out the family picture were the two big wheels—Mom and Dad. My earliest memories of them are of two quarreling people living under the same roof. I never saw them show affection toward each other. They never smiled at each other, never held hands, and certainly never kissed. Dad was always drinking and Mom was always scolding him for his derelict ways. She surely could have a sharp tongue. If Dad had not already been an alcoholic, she would likely have driven him to drink with her domineering personality. Sometimes I saw her knocking him around when he was too drunk to stand up and her frustration got the better of her. Mom wouldn't exactly hit him; she would bang into him from behind or push him hard into a chair.

Of course, that didn't compare to what he did to her.

He could be a violent drunk, most dangerous in that intermediate stage when he still had half his wits about him and was coordinated enough to do damage. When he went on a rampage, Mom was his usual target. There were times when I thought he was going to kill her.

Whatever her shortcomings, real or imagined, Mom was far and away the most stable part of my childhood. Simply put, I knew she loved me. And I loved her. Many things happened to test that love, but in the end, it made the bond between us stronger.

I'll never forget climbing into her lap one crisp autumn day when I was five or six years old and looking through the Sears Roebuck catalog with her. She told me to pick out whatever I wanted for Christmas, and I checked off all the Lionel train items. To my amazement, every one of them was under the tree on Christmas morning! That was a Christmas I'll never forget.

Mom was also the disciplinarian of the family. When I got into serious mischief, she'd send me to the willow tree to break off a branch and report back to her. Then she would give me a few good licks with the switch. While I submitted to Mom's right to administer the "rod of correction," that did not prevent me from developing strategic countermeasures.

I remember one Sunday afternoon when she was fixing dinner for guests and I kept "piecemealing" off the table—taking a piece of food here, another piece there. She warned me to stop, but I kept on doing it. Finally, she had

had enough. She sent me outside to the willow tree to fetch a new switch. I looked for the thinnest one I could find.

When I came back inside, she had me take off my shirt and walk around the table while she stood in one corner, ready to give me a good whack each time I passed by. I started off slowly, then broke into a run as I got closer to her so that by the time she raised her arm to spank me she had missed me or nearly missed me. The truth was, she couldn't move very fast. If she figured out what I was up to, she didn't let on. After I'd made six or seven turns around the table and received two or three whacks with the switch, she seemed satisfied that justice had been served.

"That'll teach you," she said with an air of finality, waddling back to the kitchen.

Dad, of course, would be nowhere around. I don't want to sound unnecessarily harsh, but he was simply a lost cause. On the couple of occasions I saw him sober, I think he had a hangover because he was quiet and didn't want to talk with anyone. Most days when he had been drinking heavily, we all tried to stay out of his way.

That is, until he turned on Mom. I began sticking up for her as early as six and seven years of age, not that I could do much except momentarily distract him. But when I got older, I'd take Dad head-on. He was a short, thin man, and when he was good and soused, I was more than his match.

It's a gut-wrenching feeling to want to fight with your father—to want to hurt him, even if it is to defend someone you love. It distorts your view of the world, with disastrous consequences; it inverts the natural order of things. Unlike most of my friends at school, I never knew the feeling of roughhousing with a fun-loving dad who enjoyed being with his son. Our interactions were limited to the work we did together on the farm and my getting between him and Mom when he got drunk and wanted to hurt her.

One day I hid under the tarp in the back of the Chevy pickup truck as he drove into town. He was heading to his favorite drinking hole, Duffy's Tavern on Coldwater Street. But I had a surprise waiting for him. I had found out about a law in Michigan that said the wife of an alcoholic could forbid a bar owner from selling alcohol to her husband. It was seldom, if ever, enforced but that didn't matter to me.

Once Dad had been inside Duffy's for a few minutes, I crawled out from under the tarp with a two-by-four I had set aside for the occasion and entered the bar. "You can't sell liquor to my dad!" I shouted at the bartender, smashing everything around me. I broke a mirror; I broke glasses and liquor bottles. I even broke a window. It was like a barroom brawl, with me doing all the fighting. My rampage didn't last long. Several of the men in the bar grabbed me from behind and took the stick of wood away from me. Dad never moved from his seat at the counter or looked me in the eye. I cursed him out in front of everyone and walked home.

When Mom learned what had happened, she chewed

me out good and sent me outside for a willow switch. It didn't seem to matter that I had been trying to protect her. "No son of mine is going to break the law," she said flatly.

"But *they* was breaking the law by sellin' Dad liquor!" I insisted.

"Two wrongs don't make a right, Jos," she said. And that was that.

But I remained unbowed.

As I lay on my bed that night, trying to fall asleep, I thought about what had happened at Duffy's Tavern. I'd done a lot of damage inside that bar in just a few seconds, but the one target I had most wanted to demolish was left untouched—my dad.

Not that I was always in the right. As I neared my eleventh birthday, I decided it was time I learned how to drive. I didn't expect anyone to agree with my decision or take the time to teach me, so I set my own plan into action. I had watched Dad drive the pickup truck enough to know what the fundamentals were, so one day when he was out of town, I took the old Chevy out for a test drive. Our collie, Laddie, came along, riding shotgun.

Everything went pretty well at first. Oh, the gears were grinding like the dickens for the first fifteen minutes or so, but I began to get the hang of it eventually. Before long I was tooling down the single lane between the barn and the main road at a fairly good clip.

Suddenly a rabbit bolted in front of the truck. Laddie went crazy. He jumped in front of me, eager to give chase.

I couldn't see a thing as he barked and thrashed about in my lap. I ran off the lane, grazing a big pine tree. That slowed me down a little but not enough. I plowed through some shrubbery and ran smack-dab into the big corner post holding the gate that led to the pasture near our barn.

The rabbit was long gone.

I got out of the truck and surveyed the damage. Part of the front grill was gone, the hood was dented, the fender was all crumpled, a headlight was smashed, and a long, deep gash ran down one side of the truck where I had hit the pine tree. I looked at Laddie and he looked up at me and whined. *No use blaming him,* I figured.

I walked over to the gate post, which had been broken clear off, and set it back in the ground. Try as I might, I couldn't get the post to stand upright; it leaned to one side like the half-broken mast of a ship. I scratched my head and wondered what to do. *I'll try to repair the truck.* I kicked and pulled at the bent and broken metal for a while, as much to appease my conscience as to accomplish anything useful, then drove the battered vehicle back to the barn. I parked it in the shed, went into the house, and promptly went to bed. It was three o'clock in the afternoon.

A couple of hours later, I heard my dad's footsteps on the front porch and the screen door squeaking open. Then I heard him walking drunkenly toward my room, his body bumping along the walls of the house. *Oh boy,* I thought. *Here it comes.*

"Jos!" he hollered. "Where are you?"

I pulled the covers over my head and shut my eyes. The door to my room opened, and I could sense Dad leaning inside the room. "Jos!" he called again, this time not as loudly. He didn't wait for me to answer, which I had no intention of doing anyway. "Why aren't you out there feedin' the calves, boy?"

I opened my eyes. "Come on, get up," he said. "You got chores to do."

I cautiously looked at him. I don't know how he had figured out where I was, but he hadn't mentioned the truck. Had he seen it yet? I threw back the covers and ran out to the barn to feed the calves.

Not long after that, I heard some banging noises out in the shed and Mom's scolding voice. I snuck over and peered through a broken window on the side of the shed. Dad was trying to repair the front end of the truck while Mom was reprimanding him for being an irresponsible drunk.

"Do you see what happens when you drink?" she said harshly. "You ruin everything! You'll never be able to fix that damage on your own! Just take it to the body shop and be done with it!"

Dad set down the hammer. He looked genuinely confused. "I just can't remember hitting anything," he said, his voice slurred.

"You can't remember? Were you that drunk?"

"Musta been."

I returned to my chores and kept my lips sealed.

• • •

Make no mistake—I was the implacable enemy of Dad's alcoholism. It made a fool of him and brought tumult and destruction into our home.

I'd do anything to humiliate him. I'd keep an eye on him in the mornings as we did our chores, and if he walked off suddenly, I'd follow him secretly, knowing he was looking for one of the wine bottles he kept hidden around the property. He had them stashed all over the farm, sometimes in the oddest places. He knew I'd break them if I found them. But I didn't always break them. Sometimes I'd urinate in them if they were half-empty, just for the pleasure of seeing him drink from them again, too drunk to know the difference.

If he was drunk and visitors were expected, I'd sometimes drive his pickup truck around the back of the barn and park it where no one coming onto the property could see it. I'd go and find him, pushing him into the barn. I'd hog-tie him to one of the wooden stalls with one rope pinning his arms to his sides and a second rope around his neck and feet. "Jos," he'd protest in a slurred voice, "I'm your father . . ."

"Some father you are!" I'd growl back at him. And then I'd leave him there for the night.

Later, when the guests arrived, Mom would send me to the door to show them in. If someone asked about Dad, I'd reply innocently, "Oh, he had to leave for a while" or "He had an appointment in town." My answers never prompted further questions. Dad was the town drunk and everyone knew it. Perhaps they figured it was better to let sleeping dogs lie.

After the guests left and with my dad still out in the barn, I'd get ready for bed and lie awake for hours, wondering if maybe I should slip out and tighten the rope around his neck a little more . . . you know, help send him on his way to eternity. But I always feared the police would put two and two together and arrest me for murder.

The police had already been to our house twice—once when I tried to drown Dad in the bathtub after he brutalized Mom, and the second time when I pushed his head in the toilet (after I had done my business) and kept flushing. Far from experiencing remorse, my hatred toward my father grew more and more intense. There was frustration, too, because no matter how much I tried to stop him from hitting Mom, it didn't seem to make any difference. If Mom pushed him too hard the wrong way when he was drunk, he would always go for her.

• • •

My one solace was my horse, Dolly. Stroking her warm muzzle and resting my head against her neck every morning always made me feel better. I suppose I was practicing a form of pet therapy for myself without knowing it. I loved to sit with her, feeding her oats and hay, talking with her about anything and everything. She always listened quietly and patiently.

I was out with her one morning, finishing up my chores, when I heard the cows mooing louder than normal and my father cursing.

"Let's see," I said to Dolly. "My guess is he's tryin' to connect a milk hose to the air pump but can't get it on. What do you think?"

Dolly looked back at me with her warm brown eyes and neighed softly. I passed her a sugar cube I had smuggled from the kitchen, from underneath Mom's nose. "Good thing he don't try to milk you, too, Dolly," I said laughing.

Then I heard another voice, a voice that sent chills up my spine—Mom. She was shouting at the top of her lungs. For a moment, even the cows grew silent as she bellowed, "You'll kill these cows if you leave 'em hooked up like this to the milking machines!" Then the cows began to moo again, but not before I heard a lone, piercing scream.

I ran to the dairy barn. Mom's screams were louder now, and I could hear my father's grunts and curses. Inside I saw the sickening, all-too-familiar sight of my dad attacking Mom. This time, he was hitting her with a rigid rubber milk hose, striking her repeatedly. Before I could reach them, he had knocked her to the ground, where she fell in the gutter next to the cows and rolled about helplessly in the manure.

The next instant, I was on him—pummeling, kicking, spitting, and cursing simultaneously. Dad stumbled forward, trying to shake his head clear. His eyes met mine for a fleeting second. Then he cursed, threw down the rubber hose, and staggered out of the barn.

For some reason, he never retaliated against me. I was still a kid and he could have waited until he had sobered up and given me a good beating. But I didn't much trouble myself with such thoughts at the time. I followed him out of the barn, screaming behind him.

"I'll kill you one day! You hear me? I'll kill you!" I threw a hammer at him but missed. "I'll kill you in your sleep! I'll put a kitchen knife in your heart and twist it side to side!"

Dad never turned around.

And then I heard my mother crying for help. She couldn't get up and I couldn't lift her. She was way too heavy for me. I knelt beside her, half-wiping the blood and cow manure from her face and crying with her.

"He don't mean it," she said, her eyes pleading with me. *Why is she trying to convince me?* I wondered. "He don't mean it," she repeated, choking on her tears. I wanted to tell her to shut up because he did mean it. And so did I. Oh, how I hated him! I wanted him dead so bad I could taste it. I wanted to do to him what he had done to her. I wanted him to feel the pain he was causing others. I would double it, triple it.

Mom's voice interrupted my thoughts. "Go get Wayne," she said in a pathetic tone. "Get Wayne . . ."

Yes, I thought. *Get Wayne. That's what I need to do.* Feeling numb all over, I stood up and ran to the house.

3

Wayne

"WHAT WOULD I do without Wayne," Mom was fond of saying. And with good reason.

Wayne Bailey did all the housework Mom couldn't do because of her excessive weight and immobility. He first came to work for us when I was six years old, essentially taking on the duties of a farmer's wife. He even liked to decorate things a bit. We didn't have much in the way of paintings or other furnishings, but Wayne could be industrious and, in a way, artistic. He put up some shelves in the living room and filled them with decorative teacups and other bric-a-brac that kind of gave the house a homey feel. He also kept parakeets, but they stayed in his upstairs bedroom at Mom's insistence.

I can remember the day we met. He was in the kitchen when Mom first introduced us.

"This one here gets into all sorts of mischief," Mom had said at the time, turning me around to face Wayne. "But starting today, he's gonna learn to obey you better than he obeys me."

Wayne smiled. He looked to be in his late thirties with a slender build and unusually long fingers. He combed his hair straight back and was neatly dressed in slacks and a button-down shirt. He took a step toward me and bent over to look me directly in the eye. His thin lips parted, revealing small, yellow teeth. He put his hands on my shoulders.

"Don't worry, Mrs. McDowell," he said. "Jos and I are going to get along just fine." Then he winked at me. "Ain't that so, little fella?"

I nodded because I knew I was expected to.

Mom was pleased. "All right, then. Now listen here, Wayne. I haven't done any dusting on top of these shelves for months. You won't have any trouble reachin' up there, I'm sure. . . ."

I left the kitchen as Mom and Wayne set to work cleaning up, pausing in the doorway for a last look. I saw Wayne putting on one of Mom's aprons and giggling. *He'd never last doing real farm work,* I thought to myself.

• • •

It wasn't farm work that needed doing that morning as I ran into the house for Wayne's help. Since he had heard all the shouting, he knew what was going on. It wasn't the first time this had happened, and it wouldn't be the last. He popped his head out of the kitchen, where he had been washing dishes, and walked over to me slowly, drying his hands on a kitchen towel and leaning down, close to my face. "It's your ma again, ain't it?" he asked.

I recoiled slightly. Wayne always seemed to have bad breath. Still, there could be a tenderness in his eyes, too—a kind of understanding. When he reached to console me, I pulled back and pretended not to notice the hurt look on his face.

"Mom needs help," was all I said.

Wayne extended his hand toward me again, this time brushing my hair back. "No use frettin' about it, Jos. Let's go see what we can do."

We walked outside and hurried toward the barn. Mom was where I had left her, but she was caked in manure from rolling back and forth in the gutter in a vain effort to get up.

Then another farm worker appeared—an older man named Shorty—and the three of us managed to get Mom to her feet. Both her hips had been thrown out of joint. This happened frequently because of her great weight, not just because of the altercation with Dad.

Shorty brought the pickup truck around, and we drove Mom to the house and labored to get her inside. Wayne called Dr. Blakeslee to come and reset Mom's hips. Meanwhile, Shorty offered to drive me to school, but I decided to ride Dolly instead. If I could have, I would have taken her all the way to the Pacific Ocean. But Dolly was a riding stable horse and had been trained never to go more than a mile and a half before turning around.

It was far enough to get me to school.

• • •

For the next several weeks while Mom stayed in bed, Wayne was in charge of the household. He didn't have a family of his own (leastways he never told us about one), but he did have a close friend, Leonard Miller. The Millers had a farm about two miles up the road. Leonard, who still lived at home, was a few years younger than Wayne and had never married.

Wayne didn't have a driver's license, so on the weekends Leonard would pick him up so they could do things together. In the summer months, he would drive his father's Mercury convertible.

"I'll be back late," Wayne would say to Mom, like a teenage son talking to his mother. "Don't wait up for me."

"Where ya headed this time?" Mom would ask, stepping onto the porch to see him off.

"Battle Creek!" said Wayne, hopping into his fancy ride.

"You goin' to the picture show again?"

"Sure are."

"What you watchin' this time?"

"*A Streetcar Named Desire*," shouted Wayne as Leonard raced the engine impatiently. "I can hardly wait!"

"Ain't you two already seen that one?"

"We like it!" said Wayne as they pulled away. Wayne waved good-bye over his shoulder.

"You two be good," Mom would say, mostly to herself, as she waddled back into the house.

Once I heard visitors who had come over to our house talking about Wayne and Leonard. It was a Sunday afternoon and Wayne was gone for the weekend. Mr. O'Brien had had a few drinks with my dad and was making comments about how Leonard Miller and Wayne always seemed to prefer each other's company.

"I think they just get along well with each other," said Mrs. O'Brien airily.

"There you go again," said Mr. O'Brien, "sticking up for him."

"What other people do behind closed doors, George, is hardly any business of ours," said Mrs. O'Brien. Then she turned to Mom. "I'm sure you'll agree, Edith."

"Yes, yes, I agree," said Mom.

"We all need a measure of privacy," continued Mrs. O'Brien, rambling on about people living in glass houses and how cultured people should not be casting stones. I had been listening from the top of the stairs. I turned quietly and walked into Wayne's bedroom. He had asked me to feed his precious parakeets while he was away. I liked feeding them, but I didn't enjoy being in Wayne's bedroom. I fed the birds as quickly as I could and left, shutting the door behind me.

Like Mrs. O'Brien, I could not say with certainty what

took place between Wayne and Leonard behind closed doors. But I could say what took place between Wayne and me.

• • •

Wayne began molesting me within weeks after he started working for my family. The first time it happened I was six years old, and I had no idea what was going on. I remember feeling confusion and shame, then excitement and pleasure, and later seething anger and a deep sense of guilt. Wayne's abuse and emotional manipulation would continue for the next seven years.

Twice I told Mom about it, but she didn't believe me, dismissing the subject as unfit for discussion. At that time in America, and perhaps in society in general, sexual abuse was hardly talked about. It was considered something best kept from the public eye—hushed up and consequently never dealt with as it should have been.

When Mom rebuffed me for telling her about Wayne's actions, I never talked to anyone else about it. I don't think they would have believed me anyway. And if they had believed me, they would likely have sidestepped the issue, hoping the problem would somehow just go away.

But it didn't go away. Wayne came looking for me whenever he could, whenever an opportunity presented itself. If I was alone on the farm for an hour or two, he became a hunter in search of his prey. If I was alone in the barn doing my chores, he'd come looking for me. Sometimes I'd wake up early in the morning with him sitting on the edge of my bed, fondling me. "Doesn't that feel good?" he'd say. Then he'd have me get up and dress for school in front of him. It was devastating every time.

Sometimes, and I know this may be hard to believe, Mom and Dad would go off on a trip together, usually out west to visit relatives. Naturally, they'd leave me with Wayne, and the warnings from Mom before they left were always explicit: "Do everything Wayne tells you to do. If I hear that you disobeyed, I'll give you a good thrashing when I get back."

"Why don't you take me with you?" I'd offer hopefully.

Mom's eyes would flash with righteous indignation. "And have you miss school? Not on your life, young man. Besides, you have your chores to do."

On the eve of one such trip when I was probably nine years old, Mom saw me looking sullen and called me over to her side. She inspected my left hand. "Is that crazy teacher still rapping your knuckles?" she asked.

I nodded. I was naturally left-handed, and Mrs. Blum, my third grade teacher, was trying to "beat it out of me" with a wooden ruler.

Mom let go of my hand. "I need to get down there when we come back and have a word with the principal. Such nonsense!" She looked around the room. Dad had fallen asleep reading the *American Farmer Magazine* and was snoring peacefully. Mom yawned and waved me away. "Go on and get to bed, Jos. It's late."

A few days later, they packed up the Chevy sedan

and drove off. I watched the cloud of dust disappear behind the car and prepared for the inevitable. With Mom and Dad gone for more than a week, there was no escaping him.

He always started by rubbing my shoulders. (To this day, I have difficulty with even well-meaning people placing their hands on my shoulders.) Then he'd kiss me on the cheek and his hands would go all over my body. I wanted to scream; I wanted to run away. But where would I go?

"Relax, Jos, just relax," he'd say in a soothing voice. "You know how much you like this."

And I hate to admit it, but there was one part of it I did like. It was the show of affection. No one else showed me physical affection, and I was aching to feel loved. I remember thinking, *If only my father were here. If only he were sober. If only he could put his arm around my shoulder instead of Wayne. If only his lips could kiss my cheek and his voice soothe my heart.* Oh, how I longed for a father's love!

When Mom and Dad returned from their trips, Mom would ask if I had obeyed Wayne. I would nod that I had. Mom would look to Wayne for corroboration, and he'd nod with a knowing little smirk. He'd stand behind me with his hands on my shoulders and his long, bony fingers dangling about my neck like creeping vines. "He was a little angel," Wayne would say in a cooing voice.

Such was life growing up on a farm in "idyllic" rural Michigan in the 1940s and early 1950s—a quiet corner of middle America boasting four seasons, green pastures, and cattle on a thousand hills. A land of peace and plenty where family included one's neighbors and friends. A place where children slept peacefully at night, secure in the safety of their own beds.

At least the majority of them.

4

Junior's Betrayal

IT WAS A SATURDAY morning in the late spring of 1951. I dressed quickly and made my way downstairs in the dark. The silence in the house told me I was the first one up. I splashed some cold water on my face, grabbed a biscuit off the stove, and stepped outside.

It's going to rain, I thought, breathing in the moist, heavy air. I walked toward the barn to start my chores. The ground was covered in mist and fog.

I probably spent too much time talking with Dolly because the chores were still unfinished at seven o'clock, when I ran into the house looking for Mom. *The chores can wait,* I said to myself.

Wayne was in the kitchen washing dishes. "Uh, where's Mom?" I asked.

"Your mom's busy," Wayne answered tersely. He dried his hands on his apron and walked into the dining room with a broom and dustpan. "She wants you to help me," he added. "You can sweep while I do the dusting."

"I got chores of my own to do," I replied.

"Chores to do?" Wayne asked, his eyes narrowing. "And just where have you been all morning if you weren't doing your chores?"

"I been busy . . . feedin' Dolly."

"An hour and a half feeding Dolly? You must not think I'm very smart, young man."

"It's not what you think."

Wayne raised an eyebrow.

"Dolly's sick," I added. "Real sick."

Wayne again looked at me suspiciously. Then he seemed to relent a little. "I tell you what we'll do," he said, putting his hand on my shoulder. "Let's finish up in here and we can go out to the barn together and see what's wrong with her."

I pulled away from him. "Naw . . . I'm goin' outside to look for Mom."

Wayne got exasperated. "She's up the hill with your dad!"

My eyes widened. "Since when?"

Wayne realized he had said too much and returned to his dusting, speaking in a nonchalant way. "She don't want you up there."

"They're moving the house then!" I exclaimed.

"Don't be silly!" he laughed. "You can't move a house."

"Oh yes you can. Shorty told me you can." I started toward the door.

Wayne glared at me. "Your mom said you need to help me clean this house!"

I looked around quickly. "The house is clean, Wayne! Good job!" And before he could say another word, I bolted out the door.

"Jos!" I heard Wayne calling after me. "Come back here!"

I had no intention of obeying Wayne. He might as well have been talking to the wall or one of his parakeets. I jumped off the front porch and ran behind the house toward the hill on the north side of the property. A big truck had been parked there for two days, and now at last, things were beginning to move into action.

In the distance, I saw workmen hauling heavy chains and tools around, while cars and trucks from town were pulling up alongside the ridge. I could see people gathering around the house that Junior had said he was going to move off the property. Everyone was shouting good-naturedly and laughing. I ran harder. This was one event I was not going to miss. No, sir. This was like having the circus come to town—only better. The circus was coming to my own backyard!

The house had been built originally for the seasonal workers who stayed on the farm several months out of each year. Now Junior was moving it down the road to his "new land." Every time the subject had come up for discussion,

Mom would begin to cry and Dad would get angry. Furthermore, there was talk of a "law suit" and how Junior was taking the family to the "cleaners."

"What's a law suit?" I would ask Mom later.

"You're too young to understand," Mom would say, crying into her well-worn handkerchief, and then proceeding to give me an explanation anyway. According to Junior, Dad had reneged on promises to compensate him for all the work he had done on the farm over the last seven or eight years. Junior claimed he had been promised several acres of farmland and the workers' house. Dad claimed he had promised no such thing, but Junior had witnesses and had taken Dad to court. It didn't mean a whole lot to me. Dad and Junior were always quarreling about something or other anyhow, and I didn't see how this was much different from the other times. What I really wanted to find out was, how in the world do you move a house? Were helicopters going to fly in, lift the house up, and carry it to its new location? Or maybe airplanes were going to swoop down and haul the house away on thick, strong ropes! I had no idea how to move a house, but I sure as heck wasn't going to miss the show!

I was out of breath by the time I reached the top of the hill. The house was already partially raised, and several of the workmen were positioning heavy wooden beams underneath the flooring. A former US Army truck was backing up in the mud, maneuvering into position to load the house on its flatbed. Then Dad appeared, stumbling around the corner of the house and shouting at the workmen to get off his property. The big, tough-looking foreman glared at Dad and told his men to "keep workin'."

Dad cursed the foreman and zigzagged over to where Mom was standing with Sheriff Reid. "Ain't you gonna do somethin' about this?" Dad asked the sheriff. "I want those men offa my property!"

"Nuthin' I can do about it, Mac," replied Sheriff Reid. (Most of the grown-ups in town called my father "Mac.") Then Sheriff Reid held up a piece of paper, damp from the drizzle, and dangled it in front of Dad's face. "According to this here court order, that house now belongs to Junior, and he has the right to move it if that's what he wants to do."

"Can you believe this?" sputtered Dad, squinting to read the piece of paper. Mom began to cry.

Meanwhile, Junior was digging up the rosebushes Mom had planted in front of the house, cheered on by his Future Farmers of America friends as well as the neighbors and folks from town. I saw Mr. and Mrs. Katzenberg there, standing next to Junior along with their oldest daughter, Jill; the O'Briens; the Bergers; the Hopkins family. There must have been thirty or more people from town, all of them good friends of the family. Everyone was smiling and laughing and having a good time. I greeted several of them. But something didn't seem quite right. They were clustered around Junior and seemed to be purposely ignoring Mom and Dad.

"Thanks for coming out today, everyone," I heard Junior shout to the crowd. "I really appreciate your support."

"Stop diggin' up those plants, boy!" interrupted Dad,

pushing his way through the crowd. Then he shouted at the neighbors, "And I want the resta you people off my property! This is family business! You folks need to go on home!"

Dad grabbed Junior's arm and tried to wrestle the shovel away from him. Junior pushed back hard, and Dad lost his footing and fell on his backside. Everyone roared with laughter. I walked beside Mom as she made her way toward the ruckus, waving her white handkerchief in front of her as though calling for a truce. No one paid her any mind. Instead, they turned on Dad, scolding him like a child as he struggled to get to his feet. The ground was slippery and, of course, he was drunk.

"Useless old wino!" someone shouted. "Why don't you leave Junior alone?"

"He's the one who made this farm what it is," said another. "Give 'im what belongs to him."

"We got you covered, Junior!" exclaimed someone else. "Take the bushes and everything else."

"It's your house, ain't it?"

The voices blurred together as I tried to steady Mom, afraid she might fall too. She had the look of someone drowning at sea . . . the resigned look of one whose strength has gone, with nothing left to do but give up and let go. The crowd smelled blood and began mocking her and Dad in the most vile language imaginable. I looked into the faces of these "good folks"—these family friends and neighbors I had known all my life. How could they be calling my mom and dad such names? Why were they being so mean, so vulgar? And why was my brother acting as though he was our enemy? It seemed the world had turned upside down.

Lightning flashed in the distance, followed by rolling thunder and the sound of approaching rain. I looked around again at the goings-on, desperately hoping for a show of pity from someone.

The rain began to fall, and I saw people opening their umbrellas. Mr. Katzenberg held his umbrella over Junior as he finished digging up the rose bushes. Mom and Dad stood at a distance, looking on helplessly as the workmen jacked up the house and made the final preparations before hauling it away. *This isn't going to be a neighborhood party after all,* I realized. *There aren't going to be airplanes or helicopters moving a house down the road, either. The real world don't work that way . . .*

I had not known love in my home, but now I knew there was no love in our neighbors' homes either. There was no love anywhere in the world. I remember thinking, *There is no hope. There is no love and there is no hope.* And then my mind went blank.

The next thing I knew, I was halfway down the hill, running toward the barn, crying and screaming. Behind me, I heard a loud cheer as the truck revved up its powerful diesel motor and began hauling the house down the dirt road to "Junior's land." With the division this created in our family, I didn't know if I would ever see my brother again.

• • •

I stood awhile just inside the barn, catching my breath. I was soaking wet from the rain. At the other end were stalls containing wheat, oats, and shelled corn for mixing cattle feed. I ran up the steps to the grain bins, passed through a large door, and lowered the door's heavy iron latch behind me. In front of me were two windows with solid wooden coverings, propped open by smaller sticks of wood. I knocked out the sticks holding up the coverings and, there in the darkness, crawled in among the shelled corn and buried myself up to the neck.

I wanted to die. Not because the "party" on the hill had gone sour; not because my parents were humiliated by false friends, or my brother had turned on his own family; but because all these things—and much more—had combined to break something inside me and fill me with profound bitterness. I was so ashamed. I felt I did not have a friend in the world.

I cursed God between sobs. Up until then, I suppose I had maintained something of a child's faith in God. Now I didn't know if He even existed. I clenched my fists and challenged Him to stand in front of me. If He had appeared, I would have attacked Him with every ounce of strength in my body. I hated God more than anything in the world. Well, more than almost anything.

I hated Dad just as much, maybe more. I cursed him over and over, as though I were taking an oath. Even now,

I figured he was probably out scrounging for one of his wine bottles instead of doing something useful. He was no father. He was a miserable drunk who just happened to have children. He'd get what he had coming to him. I'd see to that.

An hour passed, then two, three. I began to get hungry. No one had come to look for me, and it now became increasingly clear that no one was going to come. I was completely alone, and it seemed no one anywhere in all the world cared whether I lived or died.

Eventually, I struggled out of the corn bin and pushed open the door. Bright sunlight poured in, blinding me. I squinted, wondering if I might see someone there in the light. Someone who had come to look for me. My mother, perhaps. She'd be calling my name, worried that something had happened to me. But no one was there. There was only the eerie sound of wind blowing through the open spaces in the sides of the barn. I walked past Dolly and the other animals. Dolly neighed softly, as though calling me to linger a moment. I glanced at her but walked past without stopping.

There is no love to be found in the world, I remember thinking. *People put on airs and fronts because they think they're clever and can fool people with their hypocrisy. But they don't fool anyone. We're all the same. We're no better off than the animals. One day, we'll die like they do. We'll be forgotten and rot away. There is no purpose in life. There is no God.*

I left the barn and walked across the field to the house.

Whatever shred of childlike innocence that might have been left had completely, irretrievably disappeared. Perhaps it had been gone for a while and I had not realized it in such stark terms. But there was something I did understand—something hard and implacable had taken the place of innocence. I welcomed bitterness into my heart as my new best friend. I consciously abandoned—as far as I knew, forever—any notion that God cared about me. Going on twelve years of age, I said good-bye and good riddance to the Almighty.

5

High School

I THOUGHT ONLY little kids ran away from home, but when I turned thirteen, my mom left home too. I was the first to find the note she had left on the kitchen table for Dad:

"I've gone to Chicago. When I find a job and get settled, I'll send for Jos so's he can come and stay with me."

Eventually, I showed Dad the note. I noticed that for an entire day, he stopped drinking. Then he started up again. Friends of the family in Battle Creek learned where Mom was staying and persuaded her to come home after a few weeks. When I saw her, I tried to hug her around the waist, but I had to settle for one arm.

"I didn't think you were comin' back, Mom," I said. She was silent. "Don't ever do that again, okay?" I asked her.

But she didn't answer. She just kept running her fingers through my hair. She walked toward her bedroom and turned in the doorway to look at me. "I'm tired, Jos. I'm gonna lie down for a while. Help Wayne with dinner."

"Yes, Mom."

I went into the kitchen and Wayne put me to work stirring a big pot of stew. I guess I was lost in thought because I didn't even realize he was behind me until I felt his long fingers running down my back. I knew in that moment I wanted to kill him.

"Guess what I'm doing after school these days, Wayne?" I asked him.

"What?" he replied absentmindedly.

"I'm playing football."

He leaned closer to my neck to take in my scent. "That's a man's game . . ."

I whirled about and slammed Wayne up against the wall. In an instant, I had one hand around his throat and the other balled into a fist in front of his face. "Don't you ever touch me again! If you do, I'll kill you!" Wayne's eyes bulged in fear. He had seen my temper in action before. I squeezed his neck tighter. "Do you understand me?" He nodded slowly. But I wasn't done with him yet. I squeezed his neck until his face started turning blue. *Why not kill him right now?* I thought, squeezing tighter. There were several places on the farm I could stash the body.

Wayne started to wet his pants. I pushed him away in disgust. He slid to the floor, shaking and quivering. I kicked him on my way out. He never dared to touch me again. Both of us went about our business, barely acknowledging each other. A few years later, Wayne quit his job and left the farm for good.

• • •

I was happy to see Wayne go. But his departure didn't make anything better at home. In fact, I had more work to do around the house than before. Like my older siblings, I now counted the days until I could get off the farm for good.

School was a welcome break. I excelled at basketball and football, becoming quite the star during my junior and senior years. One night I scored more than forty-five points during a basketball game and was written up in the newspaper as "Josh" McDowell. The name stuck, although to my family and friends I was always Jos. In tenth grade, I began dating Sharon Tule, a relationship that continued for the remaining years of high school. My grades were solid enough, and I began pocketing extra cash by doing part-time repair work on automobiles.

I even found "surrogate parents" as a result of my athletic prowess—Dr. Blakeslee and his wife. They "stood in" at all the games because my own parents never came; my father for obvious reasons, my mother because she was too short and fat to get up and down the narrow bleachers. It was just as well. I was embarrassed to be seen with her in public.

The Blakeslees, however, were different. From what I could tell, they actually enjoyed being together. They were sharp dressers, so they made an attractive couple. Mrs. Blakeslee often wore white gloves up to her elbows and a pretty hat or colorful scarf around her head. She was slender and pretty, too, and always gave me an encouraging smile. Not surprisingly, Dr. Blakeslee was held in great regard by everyone in the community. In his years of caring for my mother, he came to know many of the family secrets, which I believe influenced the gentle, caring way he dealt with me. He was a man you could trust. They were my ideal of the perfect couple and perfect parents, and I liked to fancy myself as their son. I knew I was just fooling myself, but mentally placing them in that role took away the pain for a while and pushed me to excel.

Not that my mom didn't try to be a good parent. In fact, she tried in a lot of different ways, but nothing ever seemed to work out.

At the end of my senior year, the class party was at my house. Mom and I worked really hard on all the preparations; we had decorated tables and set them under the willow tree. Some of my friends helped me create a softball field behind the barn and we borrowed horses for the day so that anybody who wanted to ride was able to. It was meant to be a fun, relaxing day; a full day off from school to celebrate our upcoming graduation. I had one big concern, but Mom set my fears to rest. "Don't worry," she said. "He'll be in town all day. I've made sure of it."

On the day of the party, we were sitting outside, just starting to eat, when Dad came driving up the lane to the house. I could tell immediately he was drunk. Without any hesitation, he drove straight through the fence, then across the yard, through Mom's plants and shrubs, and then back across the yard and through the fence on the other side. When he finally stopped, he climbed slowly out of the truck, staggered around for a few seconds, and fell flat out on the grass.

Everyone just laughed. I ran into the house crying, and Mom followed me inside after a few minutes. "Jos," she called softly. "Jos, where are you?" She found me sulking in my bedroom. I didn't want to talk to anyone, and I refused to go back outside.

"He's had a hard week is all." I couldn't believe Mom was defending Dad's behavior.

Just then, my English teacher, Mrs. Philpot, walked in. She encouraged me to go back outside. "I can't," I said.

"Everything will be okay," she said.

"No, it won't," I said. Nothing would ever change or be okay as long as my mom refused to acknowledge that my dad was an alcoholic. My harsh measures hadn't changed him, but Mom's sidestepping was just as ineffective, if not more so.

I heard David, one of my best friends, calling me. I wiped my eyes and went out to the living room. Peeking through the curtain, I could see Mr. Redmond, my algebra teacher, leading Dad away. They were headed toward the barn from the looks of it. *I'll tie you up good tonight,* I muttered to myself.

"Jos!" cried David. "Come on out!"

I opened the screen door and strode onto the porch. All my friends were watching Dad and laughing. I laughed, too, but I was crying on the inside. I made my way to the tables under the willow tree, still laughing. David grabbed my arm and pulled me down next to him. He knew I was hurting.

"Nuthin' you can do about it, Jos. Don't let him ruin the fun."

I looked at David and smiled. He was right. Still, something about it all made me as sick to my stomach as the day that Junior moved the house.

It wasn't the only time Dad had embarrassed me in front of friends. Things had been going downhill on the farm for years, and Dad had sold off sections of land a little bit at a time to get by. Things had gotten so bad financially that he had taken a part-time job as custodian at the junior high, which shared the same building as my high school.

I did my best to avoid him, but between classes I could see him pushing a broom down the hallway or cleaning up the bathrooms. I never approached him or talked to him. He didn't exist to me there. About that time, he began attending AA meetings, but he wasn't consistent about it. I held no illusions about my dad changing. I held out no hope for him either. I wasn't at all surprised when he lost his job at the junior high for being "under the influence."

Once again, Dad had to sell off some land.

About two months before graduation, I came home from a date one night and heard my mother crying. Alarmed, I ran through the house looking for her, while at the same time looking for Dad. *If he's done anything to her* . . . I didn't finish the thought; I just clenched my fists.

I found Mom in bed, crying. Sure enough, she was bruised and swollen from another beating. As usual, she defended my dad. And as usual, I grew angry. I'd find him soon enough and do to him what he had done to her. Only worse.

Mom looked at me through her tears. "Sit down, son," she said, motioning to the side of the bed. There was something different in the tone of her voice. It was unsettling. I sat down beside her. She looked across the room at the blank wall. "Your dad has broken my heart," she said finally.

"He's broken everybody's heart, Mom. He broke your heart years ago."

Mom looked at me again, nodding silently as the tears streamed down her face. "Yes. Yes, he did. The difference now is . . . I can't take it anymore. I want to see you graduate from high school, and then . . . I just want to die."

"Cut the joking, Mom—"

"Promise me three things, Jos," she interrupted. I waited for her to continue, but that seemed to be all she had to say. She turned again to look at the blank wall. "Promise me three things," she whispered.

"Yes, Mom."

"Promise me you'll never be an alcoholic."

I nodded.

"Promise me that you won't swear."

I wasn't sure how I'd keep that one, but I nodded again.

"And that you'll be the kind of son I can be proud of."

I lost it on that one. *This is not happening,* I reasoned. *Mom can't die. Someone else maybe, but not my mom.*

"Promise me," she said.

"I promise." I gripped her hand tighter and she settled back on the bed. She closed her eyes, and after a few moments I stood to leave. She was resting now, breathing easier. *She'll be better by tomorrow,* I thought to myself. *So will Dad after he spends the night in the barn.* I walked quickly from the room, determined to make him pay.

6

Air Force

GRADUATION FROM HIGH SCHOOL was uneventful. I got my diploma, showed it proudly to Mom, and within a few weeks joined the Air National Guard with several of my high school friends. We were told we'd be able to stick together under the "buddy system," but in true military fashion, when training orders arrived, our group was broken up and my friends were sent to Lackland Air Force Base without me. That wouldn't do—we were a band of warriors and needed to stick together! I confronted the local recruiter, an Air Force captain.

"I want to be with my friends at Lackland," I told him.

"Can't be done," replied the captain, sorting through a thick stack of papers.

"Don't say *can't* to me, sir." The captain looked up at me

sharply. I added, "With respect, sir, I don't believe in the word *can't.*"

He smiled, measuring me up. "Well, there is one way," he remarked.

"Yes, sir?"

"You can enlist in the Air Force and join your pals."

"I can?"

"Yes, you can."

"I can enlist . . ."

"That's right, you can enlist."

"In the Air Force."

"In the Air Force."

I rolled my tongue around in my cheek and tried to imagine what it would feel like to pass the next four years of my life in the Air Force. I wasn't coming up with anything very convincing. The captain returned to his stack of papers.

"I'll do it," I blurted out.

The captain smiled.

A few moments later, I was reciting the oath of enlistment. Even as I spoke the words, another thought began reverberating inside my head: *This is not a good idea . . .*

As it turned out, my stint in the Air Force wasn't the ordeal I had imagined. I met my short-term goal of being with my buddies for two weeks (a ridiculous reason for joining the military, I'll admit), and once I was in the regular service, I decided to make the most of it. I had always enjoyed working on mechanical things and got assigned to the repair and maintenance of C-124 aircraft at Dover Air Force Base in Delaware.

However, the powers that be concluded there was a better use of my time than working as an airplane mechanic. My athletic abilities landed me a starting position on the basketball team, and I traveled up and down the Eastern Seaboard competing against teams from other bases. There were even a few trips to Bermuda, of all places! It was an honor that reflected well on the unit, and Sgt. Williams, my platoon leader, cut me a lot of slack because of it.

I did have to pull work duty sometimes, however. One morning as I was walking past a scaffold in the hangar where two men were working on a C-124, I heard someone shout a warning. I looked up in time to see what the men working above me had dropped—a heavy exhaust pipe. There was no time for me to move out of the way. The pipe caught me squarely across the head. Everything went black.

I woke up in a naval hospital in Philadelphia. A battery of tests revealed damage to the right side of my brain from cerebral swelling. After a month and a half of round-the-clock care, the doctors continued to observe me, which meant I stayed in the hospital only from eight to five each day. The rest of the time, I was on my own.

Sometimes I'd catch the train to Dover to visit my friends back at the base, but more often than not, I'd hang out at the USO club nearby. I was sitting with several off-duty nurses one day when I noticed a young lady I hadn't seen before. *What is that nice-looking girl doing with those old ladies over there?* I wondered. I excused myself from the table and walked over to where she was standing.

"Hi there," I said. "My name's Josh." She nodded. *Hmmm,* I thought. *Not very talkative.* "What's your name?" I asked.

"Faith."

"That's a nice name. Haven't seen you here before, Faith."

"I haven't been here before," she replied coyly, as she continued to help the women sort the donations of canned goods along a worktable.

"So why are you here? A good-looking girl like you must have a lot of other things to keep her occupied."

"I'm volunteering," she said simply.

"I see. And these ladies are . . . ?"

"Volunteering too."

I was impressed. "Volunteering. That's a good thing. Volunteering, I mean." Faith didn't answer. "You know, Faith, I hope this won't be the last time you come around here. To do your volunteer work and all."

"Oh, really? And why is that?"

"Well, you seem like a nice girl."

"There seem to be a lot of nice girls here. I just saw you talking and laughing with two of them—over there."

"Oh yeah," I remarked casually, looking behind me. "They're nurses from the hospital."

"The hospital," said Faith. "You really get around, don't you?"

"Yeah, well, I've been a patient for a while."

Faith paused, scrutinizing me. I sensed a soft spot. She was compassionate. "Just what's the matter?" she asked.

"Got a head injury. The doctors said I could have been killed. I was loading a bomb on one of those big cargo planes—a C-124. Fortunately, no one else was injured."

Faith nodded solemnly. "But you're feeling better now?"

I crossed my eyes and shook my head from side to side, making a rattling noise with my tongue. Faith burst into laughter. We chatted awhile longer, but then it was time for her to go.

"When can I see you again?" I asked her.

"Well, I don't know that you will."

"Ahh, come on. A nice girl like you? I already feel better just being around you."

One of the older ladies had now "entered" the conversation and was standing between us with a somewhat imperious air. "Faith," she said impatiently, "it's time for us to go."

Faith nodded and turned to leave. "You can come with me to church if you like," she said, walking out. I followed close behind, gathering the details about when and where.

"I'll be there," I said, opening the door for Faith and the other women. I watched them as they walked to a station wagon parked across the street. Faith turned and looked back my way before getting inside the car. I waved to her and she smiled. I was feeling good about myself.

The next morning I got permission from the medical staff to skip a day of observation and attend Faith's church on Sunday. It was a small building; I wasn't sure what denomination the church was. There were maybe fifty or sixty people there. I also met Faith's parents, the Turners, and her sister, Hope.

"Hey, if you guys have another girl," I said to Mr. and Mrs. Turner with a grin, "you'll have a Charity!" No one seemed to think that was very funny, though I did see Faith and Hope smile a little.

After church, Faith's parents invited me over for lunch. It was nice being in someone's house and enjoying a home-cooked meal. I picked up my fork to dig in when I saw Faith give me a look that could mean only one thing: *Cool your jets, Josh.* I lowered my fork and glanced at her father. Mr. Turner nodded at me, then bowed his head and said a prayer with a lot of *thee*s and *thou*s in it.

As the food was being passed around the table, Mr. Turner began to question me about my background. I told him about growing up on a farm in Michigan and being a starting guard on one of the Dover AFB basketball teams.

"And what is your relationship with Jesus Christ?" Mr. Turner asked me in an even tone as he carved a slab of roast beef with a very sharp-looking knife.

I was confused. Jesus had lived nearly two thousand years ago, if he had lived at all. "Uh, I'm not related," I said finally. "Wasn't Jesus Jewish?"

Mr. Turner set down the carving knife and gave me a penetrating look. Mrs. Turner politely changed the subject.

I showed up for church the following week and the

week after that, too, but only to see Faith. The services were boring and the minister had about as much personality as a wet noodle. I also got into some strong disagreements with Mr. Turner about religion. As far as I was concerned, Jesus was just a man who happened to become famous because of the Bible. He got into trouble with his own people and the Romans, and was nailed to a cross, and that was that. Dead and gone. I mean, religion had a place in society; I was willing to grant him that much. Religion provided a sense of order and respectability for people who needed it. But I didn't need it.

I shouldn't have been surprised when, two weeks later, Faith read me the riot act.

"My parents want me to see less of you."

"See less of me or stop seeing me altogether?"

"You really don't get it, Josh, do you?"

"Get what? I like you and you like me. I'm happy with you! I'm not a bad person, you know."

"You're not a Christian, Josh."

"Well, what am I, then? I'm not a Buddhist, am I?"

"But you don't go to church . . . unless . . . unless you want to see me."

I smiled and leaned toward her to kiss her. "Why else would I want to go to church?" I said in a husky voice.

It didn't end well that night.

Five days later—Friday, December 13—I was in my hospital room when I noticed an Air Force chaplain standing just outside the doorway.

Why is he standing there like that? I wondered. *Why doesn't he come inside?*

The chaplain kept turning his hat around in his hands. Finally he spoke up. "Are you Airman McDowell?"

"Yeah."

"I'm Chaplain Gardiner." I stiffened. No way was I going to let this man pray for me. I held his eyes in an icy stare until he looked away. *That's better.*

"I'm afraid I have some bad news for you," he said.

Bad news? What bad news could this Holy Roller have for me?

"It's your mother," said the chaplain.

"My mother?" I sat up in the bed.

"She died this morning."

• • •

The trip from Pennsylvania to Michigan seemed to take forever. I hitchhiked a good part of the way. A cold wind was blowing off Lake Erie, and snow began to fall about a hundred miles from home. I tried to keep myself warm with memories of the one person in my life who I believed had loved me, even though she had not shown it much when I was growing up. Instead, my thoughts were filled with our conversation two months before my high school graduation.

I want to see you graduate from high school, and then . . . I just want to die.

Your dad has broken my heart.

Promise me three things.

If it hadn't been my mother who had died, the doctors wouldn't have granted me leave. I was still suffering partial amnesia as a result of the head injury; I'd wake up at odd hours not knowing where I was or sometimes not knowing *who* I was.

Somehow I got home. When I pushed the old screen door open and walked into the house, it was cold, so cold. No one had lit the stove. I walked around, wondering where everyone was. I poked my head inside my mother's bedroom. The covers on the bed were partially thrown back. It looked as if someone had just been sleeping there. Instinctively, I looked behind me, calling down the hallway, "Mom?" No answer.

I went to the other rooms upstairs. Empty.

Below me, I could hear the screen door open. I remained quiet. Footsteps creaked on the hallway floorboards. Whoever it was had entered my mother's room. I walked slowly downstairs.

I saw him sitting next to the bed, his back to the doorway. The wind outside was blowing harder now, and freezing rain pelted the windows. Then I saw my father pick up an edge of the sheet and wipe it across his face.

I looked at him for a moment without saying a word, then walked outside. Dad had left the keys to his pickup in the ignition. I drove into town to ask the doctor what had happened. He told me my mom had been in bed for several days when she died. "Internal hemorrhaging," he said.

"Did you see her face before she died?" I asked.

"Her face?"

"Did you notice the look in her eyes?"

He regarded me quizzically, not sure what I was driving at. "How would you describe the look in her eyes?" I continued.

"I don't know. When I got there, she had already passed."

"I see."

"There was nothing I could do, son," he said.

I nodded and stood to leave. The doctor had patients waiting. He shook my hand, telling me how sorry he was. *Say what you want,* I thought as I walked down the sidewalk toward my dad's pickup truck. *I know why my mother died.*

I got inside the truck and sat behind the wheel. Freshly fallen snow had completely blanketed the windshield. I was enclosed in a strange, luminescent cocoon. I began grinding my teeth and gripped the steering wheel so hard it seemed I would break it apart.

"I know why Mom died," my reverie continued aloud. "My mom died of a broken heart. Say what you will . . . my mom died of a broken heart."

I looked at the empty whiteness covering the windshield. I wanted to cry. I wanted to cry like I had that night beside my mother's bed. But I couldn't. I started up the engine and drove back to the farm.

The funeral was small, held at the grave site. Mom was finally getting the peace she always wanted. Soon I was hitchhiking back to the naval hospital in Philadelphia.

• • •

Though I still suffered bouts of amnesia from time to time, I was eventually released from the hospital and rejoined my unit at Dover. At best, I went through the motions. I did not want to be in the Air Force. I had three and a half years to go and felt I was headed nowhere.

I guess my feelings must have showed. One day I heard someone calling my name in the mess hall.

"Hey, Josh!"

It was Tim Reitinger, a first lieutenant about six years my senior. He was also a starter on the basketball team. It wasn't normal for an officer to sit down to eat with an enlisted man, but that didn't matter to Tim.

"We miss you on the team," said Tim. "When you comin' back?"

"Looks like I'll be sitting out the rest of the season."

Tim shrugged. "The season's almost over anyway." Then after a moment of silence, Tim said, "I heard about your mom. My condolences."

I nodded.

"You've been going through a lot lately, haven't you?"

I felt an unwanted lump rising in my throat. I couldn't say much of anything. Tim looked at me intensely for a few moments and put his hand on my shoulder.

"My grandmother told me something once, Josh. She said that even if we can't understand why certain things happen—even bad things—we can be sure that life is more or less unfolding as it should. 'Keep peace in your soul,' she told me. 'It's still a beautiful world.'"

"Yeah, well, there's always next year," I said hopefully.

"Next year?" asked Tim.

"For the basketball team."

"Oh yeah," said Tim, smiling. "You know, I have a good feeling about next year. I think we're gonna win the championship!"

Three weeks later, on a clear Sunday morning in April, Tim boarded a C-133A Cargomaster that took off from Dover AFB on a routine training mission. Seventeen minutes later, the plane crashed in Ellendale State Forest, south of the base. Tim and three other servicemen were killed, and although a thorough investigation was conducted, no cause was determined.

I was stunned when I heard the news. *Why does one man live and another die?* I wondered. *Why do the good perish and the wicked thrive?* I had no answers but found myself wishing that I could have been on that plane instead of Tim. He had so much to live for. As for me, I couldn't see much point playing out the rest of my hand. Things were not unfolding as they should. At best, life was a cruel joke.

This cloud of despair hung over for me for several days. But it wasn't in my nature to stay depressed about things. Life might be meaningless, but that wasn't going to stop me from draining every drop out of it I possibly could. Then a few days later, word came that my platoon leader, Sgt. Williams ("Sarge" to us), had suffered a heart attack.

• • •

"You're the only one who's been to see me, McDowell," he growled from his hospital bed.

"A lot of the guys are worried about you, Sarge."

"Cut the crap. I wasn't born yesterday." Then he softened a little, adding, "Thanks for coming."

I nodded, waiting for him to say something more. He tapped his chest lightly, looking out the window. "The ticker's no good, kid, and I'm gettin' mustered out. I've been in the military for thirty-three years, the best years of my life. But there comes a time . . ." His voice trailed off. After a moment, he repeated, "There comes a time . . ."

"Take it easy, Sarge. You want me to bring you something?"

"I made one mistake," said Sarge, ignoring what I had said. "Don't let it happen to you, kid. Don't miss out on having a family of your own. That's my one regret." Sarge sat up, drawing on some hidden reserve of strength, and a little color came to his face.

"McDowell," he said, "if I'm not mistaken, you'd like to trade places with me."

"Sir?"

"I don't mean being here in this bed," he said, waving weakly around the room. "I mean gettin' outta the Air Force."

"I have three and a half years to go, Sarge. You know that."

"You make it sound like a prison sentence, kid."

"No, sir. But that's the way I feel."

Sarge nodded. "What would you do if you could get out now?"

In spite of myself, I laughed. "I always thought I'd like to give college a try, but anyway, I try not to think about it." I didn't say anything about my ambition of being a lawyer. I didn't want Sarge laughing at me.

"We got new orders from the Pentagon. We have to reduce the number of military personnel working desk jobs."

"Desk jobs? How does that affect me, Sarge? I've got a technical job."

Sgt. Anderson winked. "Who looked out for you when you played basketball, kid, making sure you pulled light duty?"

"You did, sir."

"That's what I'm talkin' about," said Sarge, nodding with satisfaction. Then he closed his eyes and waved me out of the room. I decided to let things be. Within the week, I was transferred to a desk job in the commissary but given nothing to do except stare at a typewriter. They didn't even give me paper to type on. I went to see Sarge, who was still in the hospital.

"Changed your mind?" he asked me.

"I appreciate what you're trying to do for me, Sarge. But I can't just sit at a desk all day. I need somethin' to do or I'll lose my mind!"

"Here, read this," he said, handing me a file folder from the bedside stand. Inside were my medical discharge papers from the US Air Force.

"Look here, McDowell," Sarge continued gruffly, "I'm a patriot. But not everyone is called to serve this country in the military. Find your way in life and make somebody proud of you."

"Yes, sir."

"And remember what I told you. Don't miss out on havin' a family, you hear? Don't disappoint me, McDowell."

"I'll do my best, sir."

We talked a few minutes more, and then I stood to leave. "I'll be keepin' an eye on you," Sarge said, giving me a salute. I saluted back and started to go, pausing to say a last good-bye. Sarge looked away quickly, wiping at his eyes.

"Allergies," he said, his voice muffled by the pillow.

"I'll get the nurse for you, Sarge."

"Get outta here, McDowell."

A week later, I was heading west.

7

New Horizons

I WASN'T SURE where to go or what to do with my newfound freedom, but one place I was determined to avoid was the farm in Michigan. I ended up in Chicago, near my sister Shirley. I found a job doing maintenance work on refrigeration units of eighteen-wheelers hauling meat and produce cross-country.

There were a few basic points to the job, all of which I was taught on my first day at work. A guy named Felix showed me the ropes. He pulled his car up next to a truck that had been left for servicing and began to siphon gasoline from the truck into his car. I looked around nervously. "Don't worry," said Felix with a grin. "The driver won't be back for four or five hours."

"I was thinking about the boss, not the truck driver."

Felix laughed. "The boss? Who do you think taught *me* the ropes?"

Felix proceeded with my orientation. He and another guy named Jerry unscrewed the refrigeration unit, attached it to a winch, and lifted it off the truck. Jerry then squeezed inside the trailer and began passing the bounty back to me and Felix. Hams, turkeys, boxes of steaks . . . it was a bonanza. Then the refrigeration unit was serviced and put back in place, and the screws tightened as before. Presto.

When the unsuspecting driver returned to pick up his truck, Felix and Jerry became accomplished actors with Oscar-worthy performances of being hard at work—climbing off the rig or wiping their oily hands with shop rags. They walked around the semi and inspected it from top to bottom with the concerned looks of hardworking men doing their part to keep America safe and prosperous. The unwitting driver would check the locks and seals on the doors of the trailer, sign the job ticket, and hit the road—usually fifty to a hundred pounds lighter than before. "Get over here, Josh," Felix would call to me. "Give him a nice wave of the hand to send him on his way."

"Don't forget to smile," Jerry added. We stood in the garage doorway like the three amigos.

I won't lie; I went along with it. But over time, my conscience began to get the better of me. I couldn't help remembering a promise I had made to my mother.

Be the kind of son I can be proud of.

Lying in my bed at night, I would sometimes turn my thoughts to where Mom might be. I found myself wanting to believe in an afterlife for her sake—perhaps some mysterious never-never land where she continued to exist in some way, shape, or form. There was no one to answer my futile questions, and I gradually fell asleep. Thankfully, I had worked hard enough during the day to drift off quickly.

• • •

Eventually I quit my job and drove back to Michigan. I had decided to enroll at Kellogg Community College in Battle Creek for the fall term. To save money, I thought I'd live at home on the farm and commute to classes, but Dad said no. "The electric bill will be too high if I let you do that."

The electric bill? Another lame excuse from him and good reason for me to resent him even more. Infuriated, I drove away.

I moved into a big house just a few minutes from campus with four other guys. My major was business, but my long-range goal was to go into law and leverage that into a career in politics. First, I'd become governor of Michigan, then a US senator. It all seemed clear to me. And attainable.

My English teacher and freshman counselor, Mrs. Waugh, gave me a reality check. "You have remarkable determination, Josh—more than I see in most students. It should take you far."

I smiled at her from the other side of her desk. "I dunno if you heard or not. I'm running for freshman class president."

"Is that so? I hope you do well."

I nodded confidently. "Oh, I will."

Mrs. Waugh smiled. "I do have some concerns, Josh," she said.

I straightened up in my seat.

"Your English is atrocious. Perhaps your high school teachers were not as serious about this facet of your education as they might have been. I realize farmers and factory workers aren't always expected to use textbook English."

"I did good in English," I said a little defensively.

Mrs. Waugh winced as though feeling physical pain. "Josh, you consistently use incorrect grammar. Your pronunciation is also poor. I suspect that's because your spelling is so bad." I slumped a little.

"However, if you're willing to work hard and apply yourself, I'm willing to help you."

I was willing. I knew that if I were to rise to the top of any profession, my grammar needed to be top notch. "You'll tutor me?" I asked.

"I'm willing," she replied.

"Then so am I."

I worked hard, and my grades improved. I took a part-time job at Coward Pharmacy in Battle Creek and entered the fray as a candidate for freshman class president. I was at a party every weekend, found a nice girlfriend, and bought myself a black secondhand MG convertible. Some of the boxes on my thirty-year plan were being checked off within the first six months. Things were going great.

• • •

One day as I was driving to Coldwater from Union City, an approaching car swerved out of its lane and drove me off the road. I took down the car's license plate number and called the police. A week or so later, a guy in his mid-twenties sauntered into the pharmacy and walked up to the counter.

"Hey, are you Josh McDowell?"

I didn't recognize him. "That's me," I said cheerily.

He smiled coldly. "Just a question."

"Shoot."

"You ever been run off the road before?"

"Happened about a week ago, as a matter of fact."

"Yeah, well, I'm the guy that did it." He glowered at me, trying to intimidate me. I stared right back. "The cops arrested me, idiot."

"Is that right?" I said. "So now what, you've broken out of jail?"

"I'm gonna get even with you," he hissed at me. Then he stormed out of the pharmacy. I dismissed his antics—out of sight, out of mind.

That Saturday, I was at a drive-in diner in Lakeview, a suburb of Battle Creek, when a car pulled up next to mine and the driver began cursing out my girlfriend. I looked over and saw the clown who had run me off the road and threatened me in the pharmacy.

"Zip your filthy mouth!" I yelled back.

That was all he needed. He got out of his car, came over to me, and threw a punch. I saw red. I punched him in the face as hard as I could and felt good when I saw blood running from his mouth and nose. He ran back to take refuge in his car, where he rolled up his windows and continued to curse me out royally. Determined to make sure he learned his lesson, I marched over just as he gunned his engine, trying to run me over. I jumped behind a metal post, which saved my life. My adversary plowed his car right into the post, bending it to the ground.

I ran over to the door on the driver's side, grabbed him by the neck, and started to drag him out of the car just like I'd have pulled a stubborn calf through a gate—or my drunken father, for that matter.

The parking lot was in sheer pandemonium. A waitress had called the police, and my girlfriend was screaming for me to stop hitting him. I barely heard her voice through the din. It slowed me down a little but didn't deter me. The police arrived before I could finish the job. The guy pressed charges against me—big time!

One of the policemen pulled me aside and said, "Go straight home. This is very serious." My tormentor was the son of an influential judge in the county.

Fortunately for me, one of the waitresses witnessed the whole thing and told her story to the police, who in turn relayed the details to the judge. About two days later, I got a call from the policeman who had advised me to go home. "If you apologize, they'll drop the charges."

"He started the whole thing," I protested.

"And you nearly killed the guy. I don't know if you understand what you're up against here. This kid's father pulls a lot of weight in town."

I didn't want to apologize, but I didn't want to throw away my future, either. I said I was sorry and the charges were dropped. The policeman worked things out so that nothing went on my record. But resentment and anger burned inside me. I wondered when I would explode next—where and against whom. I didn't have long to wait.

• • •

Since I was a candidate for class president, one of my strategies was to get to know as many of the students and teachers as possible. There were all kinds of social groups and organizations on campus, and I made it my business to have a finger on the pulse of each one. I created my own mental black book, where I noted everyone who could advance my agenda. I figured this would be good training for the real thing.

One day, while sitting in the student cafeteria with some of my friends, I saw the Christian "clique" waltz in. As far as I knew, they weren't an official group on campus, but everyone knew who they were and what they represented.

They numbered, perhaps, seven students and two professors, and they hung out together. When I say they were Christians, I mean they were outspoken Christians. To me, most all of us on campus were Christians, at least as far as I understood the term, but this group was different. They acted as if their faith made a difference in their lives. I smirked whenever I saw them.

Phony smiles, I thought as they laughed and chattered good-naturedly. *What in the world are they hiding?* Just looking at them riled me, and I resolved to do something about them. They were too few in number for me to worry about the political fallout my attitude might create.

When they made their way to the table adjoining ours, I sat up a bit straighter. One of the guys at my table was telling a dirty joke but got quiet when the Christians sat next to us. I asked him why he had stopped short of the punch line. Embarrassed, he made a gesture toward the Holy Rollers nearby.

"What do they care?" I responded caustically. "They probably won't even get it." I noticed out of the corner of my eye that this got the attention of the cutest girl among them, Toni. I warmed to my subject. "I mean, Christians are playing with less than a full deck of cards, right? I wonder what exam they passed to even get into college in the first place?"

My friends at the table laughed, and I launched into a little joke of my own, speaking loudly enough for everyone to hear.

"There was this man stumbling through the woods one day, when he comes upon a preacher baptizing people in the river. The preacher smells the alcohol on the man's breath, grabs him by the arm, and says, 'Brother, are you ready to find Jesus?' The drunk says, 'Sure thing,' so the preacher dunks him in the water a few seconds, pulls him up and says, 'You find Jesus?' The drunk spits out some water and shakes his head no. So the preacher dunks him under again and holds him down longer this time."

I got out of my chair, continuing with the joke while making my way over to the Christians' table. There was an empty seat next to Toni, so I sat down next to her.

"Then the preacher pulls the drunk up and asks him, 'You find Jesus yet?' The drunk shakes his head, and the preacher, feeling a little exasperated by now, dunks him under the water again and holds him down for maybe thirty seconds. One of the deacons taps the preacher on the arm and says, 'You better bring 'im up 'fore he drowns.' The preacher kind of comes to himself, you know, and gets the shakes like this . . ." I imitated my idea of a Holy Roller preacher having a spiritual spasm.

"Then he brings up the drunk, and practically shouting, says, 'You find Jesus, my brother?' The drunk looks at the preacher, spits some water out of his mouth, and says, 'Are you sure this is where he fell in?'"

I allowed myself a smug grin as people at the surrounding tables broke into appreciative laughter. Even a few people at Toni's table smiled. But not Toni. "You don't like my joke?" I asked her. She ignored me.

"Perhaps you have a better one," I continued. "Or maybe an entertaining story . . . like Jonah and the big fish?" I looked over at my compatriots at the other table. "Now, there's a whopper, boys. Talk about the one that got away! Why, that fish gets bigger every time they tell the story."

I looked back at Toni. She appeared oblivious to my needling. "Or maybe Noah and his ocean liner? You know that story?"

Another voice broke in, a grown man's voice. It was Mr. Keller, a professor of history. "Welcome to our table, Mr. McDowell."

"Nice to be here," I replied sarcastically. I looked around at the others at the table. Everyone had a kind or at least curious expression, and I felt angry again without knowing why. "What is it about you Christians, anyway?" I asked.

"What do you mean?" asked Professor Keller.

"I mean, it's like you're in another world."

"Well, I beg to differ with you there. We're very much in this world. The same world you live in."

"Well, you act like you belong somewhere else."

"Why, thank you," said Professor Keller. Others at the table murmured their agreement.

"I didn't mean that as a compliment," I said, growing annoyed and looking around at the group. "I mean, you people are always smiling or being friendly, but it's like you think you're better than everyone else."

At last Toni spoke up. "That's not true."

"No?" I challenged her.

"Not at all. We're changed people, but that doesn't mean we think we're better than anyone else."

I gave Toni a flirtatious look. "So, how've you changed? By gettin' religion? You seem to be the real thing to me."

Toni's eyes showed a flash of indignation. "The Bible says that if anyone is in Christ, that person is a new creation."

Now it was my turn to express irritation. "Oh, c'mon!" I shouted. "Don't give me that garbage!" In the momentary silence that followed, I noticed that my friends at the other table had all drifted away. I continued with my rant, "The Bible, church . . . that's just religion, and if there's one thing I can't stand in life, it's religion!"

Toni turned in her seat to look me squarely in the eye. "I didn't say religion, mister; I said Christ, Jesus Christ. And Jesus Christ *does* change lives. Even the lives of hard-headed, egotistical young men like . . . like . . ."

"Like me?" I smirked. I was getting her to lose her cool. "Jesus Christ," I drew it out, saying his name like an epithet. "Gimme a break. You don't know what you're talking about. And even if he did exist—which is by no means proven—how could a man who lived two thousand years ago change someone's life today?" I raised my eyebrows at Toni and allowed myself a half-grin.

"Well," Toni said, with a little grin of her own, "I guess that's something you'll have to find out."

"Find out? What's there to find out? Mythology is not a science, dolly."

Oliver, another member of the group, spoke up. "I have a suggestion." I turned and looked at him. He was a short fellow with thick glasses and hair standing up on his head like tufts of straw. *Here's a goofball,* I thought.

"Disprove the Resurrection," Oliver said, "and you'll disprove the claims of Christianity."

"Disprove the Resurrection?"

"Yes. Prove that Jesus Christ did not rise bodily from the dead, and you'll find a crack in the foundation that will cause all of Christianity to come tumbling down. It's just a suggestion, mind you. I mean, rather than trying to discredit all the claims of Christianity, you can take a shortcut by disproving this one cornerstone of the faith. Save yourself a lot of time and trouble."

"Now, there's an idea," I nodded, pointing my finger at him.

"I'm quite serious about it, actually," said Oliver. "Should be quite an eye-opener for you."

"Or you," I rejoined. I put my hands on the table and looked around at the Holy Rollers. They were all sitting quietly, smiling. It was exasperating.

"We'll look forward to seeing you again," said Professor Keller in a friendly tone.

I looked at the professor and the others, feeling a tinge of embarrassment for my belligerence. If I couldn't keep my temper under wraps, they'd win the argument for sure. "The name's Josh."

Professor Keller reached for my hand.

"How do you do," I said, shaking his hand.

Toni spoke up. "Next time you drop by for a visit, try to be more prepared."

"Prepared?" I replied caustically. This girl was feisty. I liked that. "Oh, I'll be prepared, all right. I just hope you're prepared to judge the facts impartially and abandon your illusions when I produce the evidence."

"And you, Josh?" said Professor Keller. I turned to look at him. "Would the same be true for you?"

I laughed hard. "I have no illusions, professor. I'm a realist."

"Just checking."

I couldn't resist a parting shot. "You know, I'd ask for you guys to vote for me in the student elections next week, but there are so few of you, I guess it wouldn't make much of a difference."

To my exasperation, they all looked at me and smiled.

These are strange folk, I thought to myself, walking off. I pictured how their faces would look when I presented my case debunking Jesus' resurrection. *Will they be smiling then?* I wondered. There was just one problem. I needed to assemble a case.

• • •

My research began, logically enough, with the Bible. The Christian coterie at Kellogg always touted the Bible as reliable evidence for Jesus' existence—that Christ was born to a virgin, performed miracles, died, then rose from the dead. But those "facts" were based on what? The Old Testament had been written thousands of years ago. How could a serious thinker consider something that old to be reliable? As for the New Testament, from what I had heard it had been written so long *after* Christ lived that it could not be trusted either.

Still, I knew I had to read the book for myself. I needed to know specifically where it was contradictory, illogical, and implausible. As I read, I noted all the miracles and claims to divinity that Jesus made. Initially, it didn't seem it would be such a difficult task to disprove Jesus' resurrection. However, the more I studied and cross-checked the pertinent references through Bible commentaries and other reference books, the more involved and nuanced the picture became. Even the doubting Thomas (the one disciple with whom I most identified) ultimately fell on his knees before a supposedly resurrected Christ and exclaimed, "My Lord and my God!"

From time to time I'd bump into the Christians, always expecting them to badger me about how my research was going. No one ever broached the subject unless I mentioned it. They were always friendly to me and seemed genuinely interested in my welfare. *How can they be so sure of themselves and their convictions?* I wondered. It galled me and made me all the more determined to prove them wrong. I thought they were all brainwashed, but by whom and for what purpose? I had to be missing the forest for the trees. Their beliefs were little more than fairy tales!

I deepened my research at the college library, thankful for any extra help I could get. I delved into books and treatises by atheists and agnostics. I resonated with Bertrand Russell's essay *Why I Am Not a Christian*, written in 1927. Not only did he call into question Jesus' existence, he had strong opinions about religion in general. "I do not think that the real reason why people accept religion has anything to do with argumentation. They accept religion on emotional grounds. One is often told that it is a very wrong thing to attack religion, because religion makes men virtuous. So I am told; I have not noticed it."

I devoured the writings of other brilliant thinkers such as Immanuel Kant, Charles Darwin, Sigmund Freud, and Friedrich Nietzsche. It seemed to me that I could quote any one of them and effectively demolish the arguments of the Kellogg Christians. But there was one overriding problem. What made the "enlightened" opinion of a famous skeptic more valid than that of someone with a contrasting point of view? At the end of the day, both were opinions. No, I needed something more than human opinion. I needed historically verifiable evidence, empirical data that would lead to one indisputable conclusion: the Bible record could not be trusted because Jesus was not who he claimed to be.

Funny how these things happen. Most of the philosophers and writers I had been reading about were from

Europe. Suddenly, an idea popped into my head. *Why not go to Europe and do firsthand research of my own?* I'd go to the sources—places like Oxford and Cambridge, London and Paris, Heidelberg and Geneva—the great libraries and museums where the original documents and manuscripts were housed.

Perhaps a bit heady for a nineteen-year-old, but hey, why not? If nothing else, I'd have a great time seeing Europe!

• • •

I didn't work out the details all at once, but I realized that to pull off a trip like that, I'd need to start saving money, more money than I could earn working part-time at the pharmacy. In general, jobs were hard to come by in the community, so I took a more entrepreneurial approach. I knew a lot of students were looking for work, and I had an idea that would create jobs. All I needed was start-up capital.

I went to a friend named Billy Connor, who I knew came from a well-to-do family in town, and told him about my big idea.

"Let's start a painting company," I said.

Billy just stared at me.

"What?" I said, staring back at him.

"A painting company?" he said derisively. "That's your great idea?"

"People need to have their houses painted," I replied.

"Yeah, and buy groceries and put gas in their cars and bury their dead."

"Look, Billy, do you know how many painting companies there are in this area?"

He didn't know, and neither did I, but I didn't dwell on that detail. I chatted away about the fortune to be made, and Billy began to weaken.

"What name would you give the company if we—or if you—started one?" he asked me.

"I don't know. We'll do *superior* work, so we'll call it the Superior Painting Company. How's that sound? And we'll split everything fifty-fifty. What do you say?"

After some more arm-twisting, Billy finally agreed, and within the week he had put up the money for ladders, brushes, rollers—the works. The Superior Painting Company had been born.

We put an advertisement in the local paper and got our first call. "I'll make a bid on the job," I offered. Unfortunately, I had no idea what I was doing, and we lost our shirt on that first house. We paid more for paint than we earned on the whole job. Within two weeks, Billy threw in the towel—er, paintbrush.

"I've had it, McDowell," he said, walking away from the job site one day.

"Billy, you can't do that," I protested. "We've bought all this equipment. Come on, man, don't give up so easily!"

But he just kept walking. "Just keep it all yourself. I'm outta here."

Once Billy was out of the picture, everything I touched seemed to turn to gold. All of a sudden, I was making good money, hiring between ten and fifteen students at a time for different jobs. And I didn't have to pay them a lot because they were thankful to have jobs.

I began to amass a small fortune.

One afternoon in early May, I got a call from a lady who owned a bed-and-breakfast in Union City. It was a three-story, Victorian-era house with huge eaves. One look at the size of the house and I knew it could keep me busy right up to the time I was scheduled to leave for Europe.

"How much will it cost to paint it all?" asked Mrs. Burns, the owner.

I had smartened up to the risks involved in making flat-rate estimates, especially for such a big job, so I gave her an hourly quote. "I'll do it for five dollars an hour," I said.

Mrs. Burns blinked in the sunlight. She was an elderly widow, and she thought I was a "nice young man." She agreed to my terms and I set to work.

A few days later, Mrs. Burns asked me if I could build a covered porch on the back of the house off the kitchen. I had never built anything in my life, but naturally I said, "Of course!"

I got Merle, my brother-in-law, to help me with the job, and we knocked it out in a few days. I promised to pay him when Mrs. Burns settled up with me. The next day, it rained hard. I was on the front veranda when I heard Mrs. Burns screaming from the rear of the house. I ran around back to see what was wrong.

She was standing in the middle of the porch, looking

up at the ceiling. Water was pouring through. I had forgotten to put tar paper under the shingles. I apologized for the error and got Merle to come out and redo the roof.

Once everything was finished—construction and painting—I drove to Mrs. Burns's house to collect my final payment. I knocked on the door but no one answered, so I walked around to the back. I found Mrs. Burns standing in the garden, staring at the house. She cupped one hand under her chin and had a quizzical expression on her face, like someone studying an abstract painting or sculpture in an art museum. I walked over and stood next to her to see what it was she found so fascinating—or disturbing.

"My house is ruined," she said, not looking at me. "Ruined," she repeated flatly, as if she were giving the "work of art" a name. I followed her gaze and saw that the roof on the porch was badly warped. I had used the wrong lumber and it had twisted and bowed in the rain. My heart sank. I couldn't afford to miss the final payment on this job. I was headed for Europe in two days.

I tilted my head to one side, then the other, and squinted as though trying to see better. "No, no, Mrs. Burns," I said. "Don't you see?"

"See what?" she asked.

"It's the house that's crooked."

"The house?" she said in a querulous voice.

"Yes, ma'am. You know, it's an old house, and after all these years, it's probably just settled onto its foundation at an odd angle. Can't you see it tilting to the left?"

"The left?"

"No, no. I'm sorry. To the right. It's tilting to the right. Squint your eyes, Mrs. Burns. You can see it better that way."

Mrs. Burns closed one eye and then the other, as though aiming a rifle. Then she took off her glasses and squinted with both eyes. Finally, she put her glasses back on and breathed a sigh of relief. "So, it's the house that's crooked!" she said with a big smile.

I nodded enthusiastically. If I did have a gift, it was definitely my power of persuasion. "Yes, ma'am, that's right! The house is crooked."

Two days later, my guilty conscience notwithstanding, I cashed Mrs. Burns's check and was on my way abroad.

8

Great Britain

I CAUGHT A FLIGHT from Detroit to New York, then took a Pan Am jet to Glasgow, Scotland. *I'm a long way from Battle Creek,* I thought to myself, smiling at the pretty stewardess taking my dinner order. I looked around and counted six stewardesses serving a mere handful of passengers. They were all businessmen wearing coats and neckties. One smoked a pipe! I reclined in my comfortable seat and looked out the window of the Boeing 707 at the cottony, white clouds floating past. I sensed the adventure of a lifetime lay ahead of me.

I landed in Glasgow and checked into a youth hostel near the center of town. After lunch and a quick nap, I visited the Glasgow University Library. After making some inquiries, I found myself in the special collections department, standing in front of a glass case containing rare pieces of papyrus from the first through third centuries AD. The old saying "One man's trash is another man's treasure" had found literal fulfillment in this collection excavated from the rubbish heaps of the ancient Egyptian city of Oxyrhynchus. The dry sands of Egypt had preserved the twenty-three fragments on display, which included administrative documents, personal letters, a collection of songs for the flute, and a portion of the Gospel of John.

I spent the next two days in Glasgow and then made my way to London, where once again I stayed at a youth hostel. The following morning, I went to the massive British Library, the largest library in the world. I knew from my research that this library housed the *Codex Sinaiticus*, or the *Sinai Book* (the earliest known manuscript of the complete New Testament). Discovered in the nineteenth century at a monastery in the Sinai Peninsula, much of the *Codex* eventually wound up in Russian hands and was purchased by the British Library from the Soviet Union in 1933.

Here I was and there it was—the *Codex Sinaiticus*—a priceless manuscript in a bulletproof glass case that allowed me to view only two of its 347 pages written in Greek. A plaque near the case described it as the oldest substantial book to survive antiquity. *Be that as it may,* I thought, *it's still a copy of a copy of a copy of a copy. And 'twixt the cup and the lip there's many a slip.* Who could know what liberties had been taken over the years with the original text, assuming there was one?

I leaned closer to get a better look at the Greek lettering on the parchment and felt a chill go down my spine. A real person had written this, probably several people working together. It was clear that it had not been written in a hurry. Everything looked carefully and deliberately done. It was laid out in an orderly manner. And it contained the entire New Testament text. If it had all been made up, or if even part of it had been fabricated, what would have possessed someone (or a group of people) to record with such painstaking detail fictitious events? To what end?

I spent the next two days wandering through the seemingly endless corridors and display rooms of the antiquities section of the museum. I saw the Rosetta stone, which had been discovered by Napoleon's army in 1799 in Egypt. Dating from the second century BC, it turned out to be the key to translating Egyptian hieroglyphics. I walked past a long procession of ancient Egyptian mummies and massive granite statues of long-dead pharaohs, thousands of years old. Statues, frescoes, coins, weapons, pottery, and much more transported me back in time to ancient Greece and Rome, Mesopotamia and Persia, Central Asia and Palestine.

The quantity and quality of the museum's artifacts were overwhelming in both breadth and detail, leading me to an inescapable—if obvious—conclusion: History was more than a textbook. Real people with real passions had lived in the past, and that had to include the people living in the Middle East who first called themselves Christians nearly two thousand years ago! They couldn't all have been insane or brainwashed or duped; yet they made the claim that the founder of their religion had been born to a virgin, performed miracles, died, and had risen from the dead!

What caused them to hold so tenaciously to these beliefs, even to the point of martyrdom? And what prompted others, who had not witnessed the original events, to follow in their steps? How could I *prove* that what they claimed to be true was, in fact, false? I needed a breakthrough.

I went to the main lobby and struck up a conversation with one of the librarians. The first thing she told me to do was lower my voice.

"Sorry," I said.

"Now, how can I help you?" she asked pertly.

"This place is so big it should probably be in Texas," I remarked. The librarian arched an eyebrow at me. I continued. "I think I could walk around in here for months and never see the same thing twice."

"Just what are you looking for, may I ask?"

I thought about how to phrase my request. "I'm trying to uncover the real facts about what happened during the life and times of Jesus."

"I see."

"How do you separate fact from fiction? That's the biggest hurdle I face. Take the *Codex Sinai . . . Sinai . . .* What do you call it?'

"The *Codex Sinaiticus.*"

"Yeah, that one. Impressive."

"Indeed, it is."

"But it's not the original."

"It's an original copy, certainly."

"My point exactly!" I exclaimed, snapping my fingers for emphasis. "A copy from the . . . what, the mid-fourth century? Three hundred years after the events described were supposed to have happened. That leads to an obvious question."

"Which is?"

"How much has it been altered?"

"I beg your pardon?"

"Altered . . . changed from the original . . . modified to conform to a predetermined outcome. I mean, how can I trust it? Why should I believe it's true when it's that far removed from the events?"

"Our former director wrote a book addressing that question. You might find it interesting—*Our Bible and the Ancient Manuscripts*." She started thumbing through the card catalog.

"Can I talk to him about it?"

"Oh dear me, no," said the librarian. "Sir Kenyon passed away several years ago."

I was beginning to feel frustrated. "Look, I've come all the way from Michigan to prove a point. Maybe there's a God out there, maybe there isn't. I don't know for a fact one way or the other."

"So you're keeping an open mind," the librarian interrupted.

"Of course I'm keeping an open mind!" I snapped. "But what I sure as heck don't buy for a minute is that Jesus Christ is divine and rose from the dead. In some ways, it's absurd to even feel the need to prove such a ridiculous idea!" I calmed myself down before continuing. "In plain English, ma'am, I've come here looking for evidence to *prove* that the Christian religion is founded on myths and fabrications—the myth of the Resurrection, the impossibility of miracles, the whole wretched movement."

The librarian's pale blue eyes widened.

"Ordinarily, I wouldn't do this, but I don't think he'll mind," she said finally, looking through a ledger on her desk and writing down a person's name and phone number. "Give Mr. Cobb a ring. Tell him Mrs. Witherspoon referred you."

I took the slip of paper and turned it around in my hand: "Alan Cobb," I said softly. I looked at the librarian. "He can help me?"

"Oh, I'm quite sure he can. He's studied the field extensively."

"He's an archaeologist?"

"A barrister, actually."

"What's that?"

"I believe it's what you Americans call a lawyer."

I was impressed. Lawyers knew how to think, how to reason. No doubt he'd help me cut to the chase and start putting some solid nails into the Christian "coffin" I was

determined to construct and bury in the earth forever.
I found the nearest pay phone and gave Mr. Cobb a call.

• • •

"Meet me for lunch at the Museum Tavern on Great Russell Street," Mr. Cobb had said after I called his office and explained to him what I was doing in London. The restaurant was a museum of another sort, built in 1730 and festooned with memorabilia spanning two centuries of English life and history. Mr. Cobb spotted me from my description and called me over to his table next to the window. He looked to be a man in his early fifties, somewhat stout, with rosy cheeks and bushy eyebrows that seemed to be in perpetual motion. After placing our orders and spending a few minutes getting acquainted, he began asking me some pointed questions.

"Do you mind if I ask your views on God and religion? A summary description, perhaps."

"Sure," I said, glancing at the waiter as he set down my plate of fish and chips. "Well, sir, the way I see it, religion is responsible for most of the ills in the world. I consider it a lie of the worst sort. A lie that gives hope." Mr. Cobb's only response was to raise his eyebrows.

"As for God," I continued, "I guess I'd say that God is a public relations myth."

"Please explain," said Mr. Cobb, digging into his steak and kidney pie.

"Well, the way I see it is that one of our early ancestors

woke up one morning in Mesopotamia or the Horn of Africa or wherever it is homo sapiens are supposed to have originated, and he looked out at the wide world around him, scratched his head, and began wondering where it had all come from. Because this early man didn't have access to a lot of information, he thought that someone like him must have started it all. But clearly it had to be someone stronger and more powerful than he was. Someone beyond his comprehension and forever unknown. And because our ancestor was superstitious, he concluded that it had to be someone mysterious. And mysterious meant sinister. Someone with the power to destroy him in an instant. Someone he needed to bow down in front of out of fear and ignorance. Voilà—God!"

"A god made in the image of man," interjected Mr. Cobb.

"You got it!" I exclaimed.

"And you've come to England . . ." He waited for me to finish the sentence.

"Well, that's a funny story, sir. I'm from Michigan in the good ole USA."

"The Great Lakes State."

"Yes, sir. Have you been there?"

"Only through books and pictures," said Mr. Cobb with a smile.

"Yeah, well, anyway, I go to a small college there and I met this group of Christians and they've bugged me to no end."

Mr. Cobb gave me a penetrating look.

"Always so sure of themselves. And yet, I have to admit they're decent."

"Decent?"

"Yeah, good people, basically. Polite. Helping others. They always seem to have a certain peace about 'em too. Actually, they are disgustingly happy."

"Never heard that turn of phrase before," Mr. Cobb demurred. "And they—what was the word you used? They 'bugged' you?"

"Yeah, they annoyed me. They acted like they had been brainwashed. So I asked them what made them the way they are, and they told me it was Jesus. Which makes no sense to me at all. Except that they really do believe that he's still alive somehow and making them better people. And the really frustrating thing is, they *are* good people. Or at least seem to be."

"And you're attracted to that quality of life?"

"No!" I snapped and reversed myself just as quickly. "I mean, sure, I'd like to have a happy life as much as anyone else, but not at the cost of committing intellectual suicide. Anyway, I pestered them about their beliefs and they challenged me to investigate the claims of Jesus Christ."

"I see. Which claims specifically?"

"Oh, you know, that he's God's Son, whatever that means; that he lived in a human body, died on a cross for the sins of the world, was resurrected from the dead, is coming again . . . And you know what? I took it on. I decided I'd show them a thing or two. But it hasn't been as easy as I figured. My research in the States carried me only so far. I think it raised more questions than it answered, and the more I studied the subject, the more I realized I needed to come to Europe to get the whole enchilada."

"I see," said Mr. Cobb, sopping up the last bit of gravy from his plate with a piece of bread.

"Mrs. Witherspoon said you'd be able to help me," I continued. "I'd appreciate that very much. She told me you've done a lot of study on the subject."

"Mrs. Witherspoon is given to exaggeration at times. But let me ask you, are you looking for answers to questions or evidence to rebut certain presumptions?"

"I'm looking for conclusive evidence, scientific proof that Christianity is, essentially, a mythology."

"Well, I don't know that I can help you."

"Oh?" I suddenly felt deflated.

"I'm not a scientist, you see."

"Oh well, I already know that. You're a barrister," I said, showing off my newly learned word. "Perhaps I used the wrong phrase when I said scientific proof."

"I don't think you did. You want ironclad evidence allowing you to prove the truth of your case beyond contradiction. But scientific proof is of little or no use when seeking to corroborate historical events."

Something told me to keep quiet and let Mr. Cobb go on.

"You're to be commended for searching, young man. How I wish more of your generation would seek until they find! But you see, scientific proof is based on showing that something is a fact by repeating the event *in the presence* of the person questioning the fact. It is done in a controlled environment where observations can be made, data drawn, and hypotheses empirically verified. And the same results can be verified over and over again. Do you see the dilemma that puts you in if you're seeking to prove—or disprove—a historical event?"

"I'm not sure I do. But my guess is you can tell me."

Mr. Cobb's eyebrows bristled with enthusiasm as he pushed his plate to one side and leaned closer across the table. "Let us say that tomorrow, or twenty years from now, someone in Australia sets out to prove that you and I had lunch on this day in 1959 at the Museum Tavern on Great Russell Street in London. Well, he wouldn't be able to prove a thing using the scientific method. In order to make his case, he would need to use what is called legal-historical proof."

He held up a forefinger to emphasize his point. "Legal-historical proof is based on showing that something is factual beyond a *reasonable doubt*. In other words, it allows us to determine the truth of a matter based on the strength of the material evidence presented."

Mr. Cobb suddenly stopped. "Your food is getting cold," he said.

I looked down at my plate. The fish and chips were untouched. I picked up my fork and started to dig in as Mr. Cobb continued. "Now, legal-historical proof depends on three types of testimony, which are oral testimony, written testimony, and exhibits."

Mr. Cobb paused again. "Try putting a bit of this on the fish," he said, passing me a bottle of malt vinegar.

"Not bad," I remarked, enjoying the tangy flavor.

"As much as I would like to travel in a time machine," Mr. Cobb continued, "they don't exist except in science fiction stories. So there's no way our Australian investigator could physically revisit this place and time in history to make his observations firsthand and gather all the necessary empirical data. But utilizing the legal-historical method I have described, and with a little legwork, he would likely ascertain the truthfulness of the event. How, you ask?"

"Yes, how?"

"Let's start with oral testimony. That lady across the way—don't look now, but she's been watching you from the moment you entered the room. Not only can she testify that you and I had lunch in this restaurant, I would not be at all surprised if she keeps a diary. If her diary were found and you were mentioned in it, that would add written testimony to her verbal description. But let's not rest our case on her alone. Consider the waiter."

I glanced over at a nearby table where our waiter was serving drinks to several patrons. "Men in his profession develop the habit of remembering all sorts of useless information," Mr. Cobb elaborated. "He will undoubtedly recall that you're an American by your accent and that you asked him for a recommendation off the menu, prompting him to suggest the fish and chips, his own personal favorite. How is it, by the way?"

"It's good," I said, my mouth full of food. Mr. Cobb nodded with satisfaction.

"Then, too, I'll remember you quite well and be fully capable of writing a summary of the event and giving oral testimony."

"And I'll have an 'exhibit' with this receipt," I interrupted, reaching for the bill.

With surprising quickness, Mr. Cobb whisked the check away before I could take it. "I'll hold on to the material evidence for now," he said with a twinkle in his eye. He glanced at his watch. "But dear me, I really must be going. Why don't you come along to my office? We'll continue our discussion on the way."

I nodded, grateful that he was paying the bill.

• • •

Mr. Cobb's law office was located on the west side of London at the Honourable Society of Lincoln's Inn, one of the four historic inns of court where London barristers trained and had offices. Each inn was spread across several acres of prime real estate, similar to an "Oxbridge" college layout with large halls, a chapel, grand libraries, well-kept gardens, and private chambers for the barristers.

I waited in the anteroom for about half an hour until Mr. Cobb appeared in the doorway of his chambers. "Care to accompany me down to Old Hall?" he asked. Without waiting for me to answer, he strode off vigorously. I hurried to catch up.

Old Hall was a high-ceilinged room approximately seventy feet long by thirty feet wide with well-worn hardwood floors. I learned that it had seen centuries of use for traditional holiday feasts as well as court cases, and that it was now used primarily as a moot courtroom and lecture hall. As we entered, I saw several barristers pacing back and forth in pairs and talking. Mr. Cobb signaled me to accompany him as he thrust his hands behind his back and joined their ranks.

"I'm going to ask you some questions, lad. And I want you to answer them as best you can. In so doing, I hope to point you in the right direction insofar as your research is concerned. Agreed?"

I nodded.

"Now then, how would you describe the Bible? I'm not asking you what it represents symbolically to mankind or Christianity or any of that. I'm just asking for a physical description."

"It's a book. It's from the Latin word *biblia*, which derives from the Greek word for 'scroll.'"

"Excellent. Anything else you can tell me about it?"

"Well, it's actually more than one book. It's a collection of manuscripts from different authors over the centuries. The various manuscripts were put together under one cover by a bunch of big shots at a church meeting in the fourth or fifth century."

Mr. Cobb brushed off my irreverence. "And do you

know how many copies of the Bible, or portions thereof, have come down to us through the centuries?"

I sensed a trick question. "No sir, I don't."

"The current number exceeds twenty-two thousand, with new discoveries being made regularly." Mr. Cobb glanced at me. "You're not impressed."

"Should I be?"

"Actually, you should. Whenever we study writings from antiquity, the more copies we have at our disposal, the better equipped we are to determine the contents of the original. Much like a witness to an event. If there is only one witness, we must allow for exaggeration or personal agenda or just faulty memory creeping in, resulting in a muddying of the waters. On the other hand, if there are numerous witnesses to the event and they all agree on the main points, how likely is it that they *all* got it wrong?"

"Not likely, I suppose."

"Quite so."

"Where I take issue, though, is the period of time between the occurrence of the events and the description of the events—the historical record, if you will. How can we know that what we're reading today is what was actually written in the first place?"

Mr. Cobb nodded. "An understandable objection. So let's address it. What tests would you use for measuring the accuracy and reliability of any piece of historical writing?"

"Tests?"

"Yes, let's be fair. How would you measure the accuracy

of *The Iliad*, for example, or the *Histories* of Herodotus? You realize all we have to go on are copies."

We had reached one end of the hall. Mr. Cobb turned and walked back the other way, continuing with his line of reasoning. "Let me put it to you another way. Do you know how many copies of Plato's writings have found their way to the twentieth century?"

"I don't know, but my guess is you can tell me."

I saw a twinkle in Mr. Cobb's eyes. "A total of seven."

"Seven copies? Is that all?"

"And the earliest copy has been dated to approximately AD 900, twelve hundred years *after* Plato died. With such a long time span between his death and the only known copies of his writings, it's not difficult to understand how someone might have trouble believing Plato wrote the words attributed to him. Or that he even lived, for that matter!" Mr. Cobb looked at me with upraised eyebrows. "But perhaps I assume too much. Perhaps you're already of the opinion that Plato is a fictional character."

I was startled. "Me?"

Mr. Cobb nodded.

"Plato . . ." I said, clearing my throat. "No, he must have lived. I've never heard anyone question that before. Have you?"

"There are always those on the fringe about most any subject, I suppose. But no, I consider it a safe bet that Plato was a real person, though his actual name was Aristocles."

"I didn't know that."

"Let's take a look at another writer from antiquity, shall we?"

"Who would that be?"

"Oh, I don't know. How about Julius Caesar?"

"'I came, I saw, I conquered,'" I quipped.

Mr. Cobb nodded. "A remark attributed to Caesar by the Greek historian Plutarch. He didn't actually hear those famous words himself, of course; rather, he wrote about Caesar more than a hundred years after the fact, an example of establishing the truth of a matter by means of legal-historical proof." Mr. Cobb tapped his chin with the fingers of one hand. "The words themselves were spoken, as I recall, before the Roman senate as Caesar described his surprisingly swift victory over Pharnaces II of Pontus in 47 BC."

I couldn't help but stare at Mr. Cobb. How could he possibly know so much about everything? Just then, we passed two barristers walking in the other direction.

"Cobb," said the taller of the two, nodding politely.

"Whitacre," replied Mr. Cobb just as politely, nodding back. We walked on a few more moments and Mr. Cobb turned to me. "What was I on about, lad?"

"You were talking about Caesar. How he was a writer, which surprises me. I thought he was a general."

"Ah yes! Well, he was a general, of course, but also a writer who composed his *Commentaries on the Gallic War* between 58 and 50 BC. Lively reading—I highly recommend it. However, you might be wise to question its reliability on certain matters."

"Why is that?"

"Its manuscript authority rests on ten copies, the earliest of which surfaced a thousand years after Caesar died. The same thousand-year gap applies to the works of the Roman historian Tacitus, while fourteen hundred years is the time lapse between Aristotle's death and the earliest known copies of his writings. But I digress. You want to refute the claims of Christianity, not call into question the existence of men from the distant past or the assumed factual nature of their written works."

"Nonetheless, Mr. Cobb, please finish your point."

"My point. Yes, my point!" Mr. Cobb's cheeks flushed even more. "When we compare the New Testament to these other ancient texts, we find documents that are better preserved, more consistent, and more numerous than any other ancient manuscripts in our possession today. Not to mention that they are considerably closer to the original sources by many hundreds of years. And because the copies are so numerous—remember, I mentioned that there are more than twenty thousand—they can be cross-checked for accuracy. No, lad. If critics wish to disregard the reliability and accuracy of the Bible, the New Testament in particular, then they must also disregard every other piece of writing from antiquity. Even more so, I should say. Are you prepared to do that?"

Before I could reply, Mr. Cobb said, "Because that is surely the logical outcome if you approach the subject with an open mind."

"I'll admit I started out questioning whether Jesus even existed," I said. "I'm willing to concede that point now. Historians like Pliny wrote about him, as did Tacitus, and they were no friends of Christianity. So, yeah, he lived. And I have to admit you also give compelling reasons to accept the authenticity of the Bible we read today. But no matter how you slice it, so much of it still flies in the face of all that is logical or even possible."

"You refer to the miracles, I suppose."

"Call 'em what you will."

"That Jesus walked on water, raised the dead to life . . ."

"All of that and more. How can I believe any of it?"

"Apart from faith in God, you mean."

"Well, let me ask you, Mr. Cobb. You're obviously a very educated man. Do you believe that all the miracles in the Bible really happened?"

"I do," said Mr. Cobb simply.

We walked on for a few moments in silence, except for the creaking of the floorboards. I could hear rain falling outside and the muted conversations of the other barristers in the room. I suddenly thought of Mrs. Witherspoon and how she had mentioned she knew someone who might help me in my research. I had thought I would find an ally, a skeptic like myself. Clearly that was not the case with Mr. Cobb. But he was a thinker and a serious student of the subject. I had to respect that.

I broke the silence. "What if . . ."

"Speak your mind, young man."

"I'm not sure how to put it, but what if the early church deliberately created a mythology around Christ? A party line, so to speak."

Mr. Cobb was engaged. "Go on."

"What if Jesus never claimed to be divine but was just a good man who believed in peace on earth, and the whole Christian religion was created to control the masses by turning Jesus into a god the people could worship? Especially when the Emperor Constantine converted to Christianity and subsequently forced everyone in the Roman Empire to adopt the new religion."

"And you find that theory more plausible than Jesus being divine and performing miracles."

"Well, yes, sir, I do. Honestly, I do."

"It's good to be honest—with yourself and others."

Now I was energized. "And the point you make about all the copies of New Testament manuscripts. Does that really prove anything? Maybe the copyists were writing the official version that the church wanted preserved. Maybe earlier versions carrying a different story were suppressed or discredited, then finally forgotten."

Mr. Cobb gave me a penetrating look. "Reasonable points on the face of it. And I can rebut each one if you like."

"I'm sure you can," I said, trying to hide my exasperation.

"But let me ask you a personal question first."

"Shoot."

"Would you be willing to die for a lie?"

"Huh?"

Mr. Cobb repeated his question. "Would you be willing to die for a lie?"

"No, I can't imagine I would."

"Yet those first believers in Jesus were willing?"

I was momentarily at a loss for words. "I don't see how we can know the answer to a question like that. Again, you're speculating about something that would have happened nearly two thousand years ago."

Mr. Cobb continued walking, head down. "As we've established previously, all history is essentially knowledge of the past based on testimony. In this instance, the testimony was corroborated by the transformed lives of the apostles and early followers of Jesus. They willingly suffered torture and martyrdom because they were convinced of Christ's deity and His resurrection. They were unwilling to deny what they knew to be the truth."

"I don't want to be disrespectful, sir . . ."

"Carry on, lad."

"Well, many people have died for a lie or a cause they believed in. What does that prove? Look at the kamikaze pilots in World War II."

"I understand." His eyebrows were rising and falling like two flags in a stiff breeze. "But tell me this, would you be willing to die for something that you *knew* was a lie? Something that you absolutely knew was a fraud, false beyond question?"

Mr. Cobb did not wait for me to answer. "When Jesus was arrested and crucified, the disciples ran and hid. They feared for their lives. Their beloved Messiah was no deliverer after all, it seemed. No, their cherished dreams had been dashed into a thousand pieces as He died in agony on that cross. Then a few days later, something unanticipated happened, something so monumental that these same cowards became heroes overnight. They emerged boldly in the public square, and under the nose of the same people in Jerusalem who had arrested and executed Jesus, they preached a risen Lord. They were given the command to cease and desist. They did not. They were thrown in jail and forbidden to speak in His name. But they chose to obey God rather than men. Later, they were flogged and beaten. Some were stoned and crucified. Others were beheaded. But nothing on earth had the power to keep them from preaching and teaching what they had seen and heard with their own eyes and ears. They were no more willing to die for a lie than you or I would be. That can mean only one thing to me."

We stopped in the middle of the hall. I looked at Mr. Cobb and wondered if he was feeling okay. He was staring straight ahead and his lips were trembling. He rubbed at his eyebrows, then shut his eyes. I reached out and touched him on the arm. He sighed deeply, then turned and looked at me, blinking away what seemed to be tears. After a moment, he began walking again, and I drew closer to hear his next words.

"Apart from Jesus rising from the dead and appearing to His followers in bodily form, as the Bible describes in detail, there is no accounting for what they did or the courageous way they subsequently lived."

Mr. Cobb and I continued talking, and by the end of our time together, I felt we had walked for miles. It was evening and the hall was empty when we finally parted.

• • •

I would spend another two days in London with Mr. Cobb. I can't begin to tell you the number of times we paced the length and breadth of Old Hall discussing Jesus, the Bible, ancient history, and Christianity. We also revisited the British Museum to examine the astounding breadth of academic research available there, which I grudgingly began to admit lent credence to the early writing of the New Testament, a mere fifty or sixty years after the events.

No subject was off-limits between us, and we began to focus on the subject of Jesus' resurrection. I mentioned the challenge that Oliver, the Christian student at Kellogg, had given me. *Prove that Jesus Christ did not rise bodily from the dead, and you'll find a crack in the foundation that will cause all of Christianity to come tumbling down.*

Mr. Cobb and I examined the "wrong tomb theory," the idea that the disciples had gone to the wrong tomb looking for Jesus—picking the first empty tomb they came across—and they began to spread the myth that He had risen.

"That one *is* full of holes," I had to admit to Mr. Cobb.

"The easiest way to debunk it would be to produce the corpse, which I'm sure anyone who wanted to quell the sect would have been more than willing to do."

Then there was the "hallucination theory," which held that the appearance of Jesus after the Resurrection was an illusion or a hallucination. Mr. Cobb and I went back and forth on that one. Maybe the hallucination theory would be plausible if it affected only one or two people. But how about the more than five hundred people mentioned by the apostle Paul who saw the same thing simultaneously? And what about followers who never claimed to see Jesus either bodily or in a hallucination? What accounted for their manic loyalty to their dead Messiah? No, the hallucination theory was not a convincing argument; it seemed more like a poor excuse.

We talked through the pros and cons of the "swoon theory," postulated by a German theologian named Karl Friedrich Bahrdt, who claimed that Christ must have fainted on the cross rather than actually dying, and then later was revived in the tomb.

Mr. Cobb quickly put that theory to rest. "If Jesus survived the Roman flogging and crucifixion that followed, He would have been so weakened and pathetic looking He could hardly have inspired the reverence and worship of His disciples!"

There was also the "stolen-body theory" and the "moved-body theory," as well as the "copycat theory," which claims that the main tenets of Christianity were adapted from the Greco-Roman mystery religions. We examined each theory's flaws, dismissing each one handily. Of course, that didn't mean I accepted that Jesus' resurrection was a historical fact. It was still too incredible and hard for me to believe! To my mind, there had to be an explanation apart from his "divinity."

Finally, we decided to set aside the discussion of the Resurrection for the time being and began exploring the question of what kind of man Jesus must have been during His lifetime. Was He just a great moral teacher like Buddha or Confucius or Lao Tzu? Surely their moral qualities and wisdom had equaled that of Jesus. If the only words of Jesus that had survived were those from His Sermon on the Mount, He would at least be their equal—if not their superior. But He had claimed to be something more. He had claimed to be God.

Mr. Cobb introduced me to the writings of C. S. Lewis who, interestingly enough, had once been an agnostic. He showed me the turning point in his book *Mere Christianity*, where Lewis wrote,

> I am trying here to prevent anyone saying the really foolish thing that people often say about Him: "I'm ready to accept Jesus as a great moral teacher, but I don't accept His claim to be God." That is the one thing we must not say. A man who was merely a man and said the sort of things Jesus said would not be a great moral teacher. He would either be

> a lunatic—on a level with the man who says he is a poached egg—or else he would be the Devil of Hell. You must make your choice. Either this man was, and is, the Son of God: or else a madman or something worse.

Back and forth the discussion went; there seemed no end to it. I seemed to always have an objection. For every "fact" and piece of evidence Mr. Cobb produced, I introduced a doubt, a question, a misgiving. When it was finally time for me to leave London, I think we were both relieved.

I said my final good-byes in the beautifully kept gardens of Lincoln's Inn.

"Where will you be going from Cambridge?" Mr. Cobb asked me.

"I'll probably shoot over to Oxford."

Mr. Cobb nodded. "It's worth the visit. When you leave Oxford, I'd like you to head north to Manchester. The John Rylands University Library. There's a fragment on display there from St. John's Gospel."

"I'll do it, sir."

Mr. Cobb nodded with satisfaction and took an envelope out of his coat pocket. "Here are the names and addresses of two friends on the Continent—Dr. Sauer in Heidelberg and Professor Zehnder in Geneva."

"Thank you, sir!"

"I've already given them a ring letting them know you

might be stopping in. They both are experts in archaeology and linguistics. And they speak English."

We stood there a while longer. It was a beautiful summer morning. I extended my hand. "Thanks for all your help, Mr. Cobb. You've given me a lot to think about."

Mr. Cobb grew quiet. "I don't know that I've convinced you of anything. Believe it or not, my major aim was to help you examine things for yourself—with an open mind."

I nodded. "I realize that. And you've given me so much of your time—I'm glad you're not billing me by the hour!"

Mr. Cobb laughed heartily. We shook hands a final time and I walked away. My final glimpse of Mr. Cobb was of him bending over to smell some beautiful peach-colored roses. I smiled and stepped through the arched gate to Newman's Row. A few minutes later, I found myself caught up in the jarring, pell-mell rush of Holborn Street.

I would sift through the wealth of information Mr. Cobb had passed on to me for a long time. However, it wasn't the amount of knowledge he had disseminated that impressed me the most. It was the man himself, the strength and courage of his convictions. Walking down the stairwell to catch the Tube, I wondered what new adventures lay ahead. I looked at my watch. I needed to get to the Liverpool Street station for the 9:30 train to Cambridge.

9

The Journey Continues

AT THE UNIVERSITY LIBRARIES of Cambridge and Oxford, I narrowed my studies to the writings of skeptics who later became Christians. In addition to C. S. Lewis's *Mere Christianity* and *Miracles*, I read Frank Morison's *Who Moved the Stone?*, first published in 1930. Frank Morison was the pseudonym used by Albert Henry Ross, an English freelance writer. I was intrigued that Morison had developed his book from a short paper he wrote to disprove the Resurrection.

This sounds familiar, I said to myself, settling down in a comfortable reading chair at the Bodleian Library in Oxford. The book was well written and moved quickly, and I was especially struck by Morison's conclusion: "There may be, and, as the writer thinks, there certainly is, a profoundly historical basis for that much disputed sentence in the Apostles' Creed—'the *third day* He rose again from the dead.'" He definitely had my attention.

I devoured the works of other individuals whose scholarship elicited my grudging respect—men like Lord Lyttelton and Gilbert West. Both had been professors at Oxford in the 1740s, sharing the conviction that Christianity was a "tale gone mad" and deciding to work together to discredit it completely. Lyttelton set out to prove that Saul of Tarsus never converted to Christianity, while West sought to prove the fallacy of Christ's resurrection. When they came together later to compare their findings, they were shocked to discover that each had come to the opposite conclusion! In short order, they both became ardent followers of Christ. Lord Lyttelton would write, "The conversion and apostleship of Saint Paul alone, duly considered, is, of itself, a demonstration sufficient to prove Christianity to be a Divine Revelation."

Another fascinating person was professor Thomas Arnold, the former history chair at Oxford who wrote the famous volumes entitled *History of Rome*. A longtime skeptic of Christianity, he would come to a striking admission:

> I have been used for many years to study the histories of other times, and to examine and weigh the evidence of those who have written about them, and I know of no one fact in the history of mankind which is proved by better or fuller evidence of every

sort . . . than the great sign which God hath given us that Christ died and rose again from the dead.

Finally, I examined the life and writings of Dr. Simon Greenleaf, professor emeritus of law at Harvard University and a renowned skeptic. His three-volume classic of American jurisprudence, *A Treatise on the Law of Evidence*, was a standard textbook for law students throughout the nineteenth century. A brilliant lecturer, Dr. Greenleaf often mocked Christianity in his classes. One day some of his students challenged him to apply the laws of legal evidence he had developed to the case of Christ's resurrection. After much persuasion, Greenleaf took on the task in the form of a book with the lengthy title of *An Examination of the Testimony of the Four Evangelists, by the Rules of Evidence Administered in the Courts of Justice.* After carefully examining all the information available to him, Greenleaf concluded that the facts, impartially judged, spoke for themselves. He wrote, "It was impossible that the apostles could have persisted in affirming the truths they had narrated, had not Jesus actually risen from the dead."

All well and good, I thought, taking a few notes and pushing the book to one side. *No doubt Dr. Greenleaf was a great thinker. But how could he, or any man, claim to have a corner on the truth?*

I walked down to the library's tearoom for lunch. A Gutenberg Bible from 1455 was on display. I couldn't understand the Latin text, but I couldn't take my eyes off it either. Questions swirled in my mind. *What is truth anyway? Can it ever be found?*

After spending five days in Cambridge and Oxford, I caught a train to Manchester, 125 miles to the north. I had a promise to keep. I asked for directions to the John Rylands University Library on Oxford Road. When I arrived, a security guard was kind enough to take me directly to the glass case containing the fragment from the Gospel of John that Mr. Cobb had wanted me to see. It dated from early in the second century and was written by John, the "disciple whom Jesus loved" (John 21:7).

A translation of John 18:37-38 was next to the Greek text:

> "I have come into the world to testify to the truth. Everyone who is of the truth hears my voice." Pilate said to him, "What is truth?" And going out again to speak to the Jews, he said to them, "I find no fault in him."

I took a few seconds to read the translation. An hour or so later when it was time for the museum to close, I was still standing by the glass case. It was as if something heavy lay on my shoulders, keeping me rooted to the spot. The guard who had taken me to the display put his hand on my arm and quietly showed me out.

After a quick bite, I wandered the streets of Manchester for the next several hours, reflecting on how my cynical, halfhearted undertaking to disprove the Resurrection and put the Kellogg Christians in their place had evolved into something more serious than I could have imagined.

"Just what are you trying to prove?" I spoke aloud, walking across St. Peter's Square toward Bishopsgate and the youth hostel where I was staying. It had begun to drizzle, and a light fog made everything otherworldly. I turned my coat collar up against the rain and plunged my hands deep into my pockets.

My thoughts drifted to the time I had hidden in the grain bin after the debacle between Junior and my parents when the house on the hill was moved. I had cursed God and sworn to be His enemy. Because of so many devastating things that had happened in my life, I had become convinced that if there was such a thing as a Higher Power (call Him "God" if you like), He derived a sadistic pleasure in watching human beings suffer. From the age of eleven, I began to push God out of my life so that by the time I reached adulthood, I considered anyone who claimed to have a relationship with Him to be a fool. I wanted nothing to do with their God; I wanted nothing to do with their Lord and Savior. Until now. Four thousand miles from home and all alone, I was beginning to feel that somehow, in spite of all my prejudice, this God of the Christians at Kellogg Community College might be more real than I had imagined. Even more remarkable was the thought that He might, just might, want to have something to do with me after all!

Was I losing my mind?

Jesus' words in the Gospel of John had unnerved me. "Everyone who is of the truth hears my voice." Was I beginning to hear His voice coming down to me over the centuries? I had to laugh. *You know, Josh, you never have been the same since you got banged on the head by that exhaust pipe in the Air Force.*

It was time to go to France. Maybe the question would be settled there.

• • •

I took a train from Manchester the next day and bought a ticket to Paris on the Night Ferry, an international sleeper train that left London's Victoria Station each evening at nine and arrived at Gare du Nord in the heart of Paris eleven hours later.

Early the next morning, I walked down the Avenue des Champs-Élysées, alongside the Seine River, and over to the Eiffel Tower. I was an American in Paris. All that was missing was the music and the girl.

I spent nine days in France, immersing myself in all the sights of Paris, including two days at the Louvre, a day in Versailles, and three days in Lyon, home to a surprising selection of museums located in beautiful buildings within Lyon's historical center.

From Lyon it was a scenic train ride to Geneva in the French-speaking part of Switzerland, where I met Mr. Cobb's friend, Professor Yves Zehnder. We met on the campus of the University of Geneva, where he taught theology. Just as with Mr. Cobb, the professor and I discussed an array of subjects. Given our setting and the professor's area of expertise, I learned much about the history of Christianity over the centuries, including the Protestant Reformation and its proponents, Martin Luther and John Calvin.

Professor Zehnder also helped me better understand textual criticism in relation to the Bible, as well as the tools that textual critics use to identify the most reliable manuscripts while at the same time removing transcription errors that may have worked their way into the texts. "The end result is a Bible we can put our faith in as the unadulterated Word of God," he said. By the time he sent me on my way north to Germany, I carried a grudging admiration for yet another critical thinker who didn't balk at the supernatural.

In Heidelberg, I met up with Mr. Cobb's other friend, Dr. Heinrich Sauer. He was a very tall man with thinning hair and deep blue eyes. He invited me to join him on the Philosophenweg (Philosophers' Walk), a rambling, two-hour climb up the southern side of the Heiligenberg (Saints' Mountain).

Dr. Sauer surprised me by not broaching the subject of Christianity or the Bible initially. He wanted to know about me—where I had come from and what my goals were in life.

"I want to be a lawyer one day," I told him. "After that, I've thought of entering politics."

"I have a joke for you," said Dr. Sauer with a serious expression. "Why did the lawyer cross the road?"

"I have no idea."

"To get to the car accident on the other side!" Dr. Sauer said, roaring with laughter.

When I didn't laugh, he slapped me on the back. "It's a joke! Do you get it?"

I smiled and nodded. *Pretty lame!* Dr. Sauer slapped me hard on the back a second time, and I coughed.

"I get it! I get!" I shouted, holding my hands up in a sign of mock surrender. "Very funny!"

"Very funny, yes?" repeated Dr. Sauer.

As we hiked up the mountain, the man's serious, caring side showed. He was a good listener, and an hour into the climb, I had told him most of the pertinent details of my troubled childhood.

"Alan didn't tell me this part of your story," said Dr. Sauer. "Only that you were a seeker of the truth."

"I guess I didn't tell Mr. Cobb much about my personal life, but for some reason I've told you."

Dr. Sauer nodded. We had reached a point on the path with benches where we had a clear view of Old Town and Heidelberg Castle across the Neckar River. It was picture perfect in the late afternoon sun. We sat silently for a moment, enjoying the sight.

"Josh, if I may ask you a question," said Dr. Sauer somberly.

"Go ahead, sir."

"Have you considered how your perception of our heavenly Father might have been affected by the difficult experiences you had with your earthly father?"

I didn't respond right away. "You need to understand that I don't pretend to believe in God," I said finally.

"In the Bible, He is called our Father. Our heavenly Father. He loves and accepts us as we are."

"Like I said, I don't pretend to believe."

Dr. Sauer didn't push things further. "Tell me more about your search," he continued gently. "A search for truth, I take it?"

"Well, I don't know about that," I lied, laughing. "I think I'm just trying to keep pace with Mr. Cobb's questions and different lines of reasoning."

"And what perplexes you now? Do any of Alan's questions for you remain unanswered?"

I hesitated. In one sense, the answer was no. There really were no more questions to ask or answers to be given. At least none that I could think of. But I didn't want to say that. "Mr. Cobb has given me a lot to think about," I said simply.

"The final step toward God can only be a step of faith," said Dr. Sauer, looking at me intently. "Faith springs from trust; trust emanates from love. And God is love."

"Well, I still have questions about the Bible," I said, uncomfortable with where the conversation was heading. "Especially the New Testament."

"Such as?"

"I have a lingering doubt that what we read today is the

same as the original." In truth, I had no such doubt; I was trying to make conversation. "I mean, how can we know for sure when all we have to go by are handwritten copies?"

Dr. Sauer nodded vigorously. "Oh, I'm with you."

"You are?"

"In a manner of speaking, yes. You see, we could throw away all the copies of the New Testament ever written and reconstruct all but eleven verses by drawing on the writings of the early church fathers, men like Clement, Ignatius, Polycarp, and others. They all quoted liberally from the New Testament in their original works."

"And they lived—let me guess—in the first and second centuries."

Dr. Sauer smiled. "I believe you Americans say 'bingo'?"

"Yeah," I nodded, smiling. It was hard not to like Dr. Sauer. "Yeah, we say 'bingo.'"

"Farther up the mountain are the ruins of St. Michael's. Shall we have a look?" asked Dr. Sauer.

"What is it? Is it a castle?"

"It's a monastery from the eleventh century. We can reach it by staying on our path. Shall we?" he asked, standing.

"The Philosophers' Way." I followed Dr. Sauer. "*Der Philo . . . soph . . . enweg.*"

"*Ja, sehr gut!*" exclaimed Dr. Sauer, obviously pleased at my effort to speak even broken German.

"Why is it called that, anyway?"

"Over the centuries, our poets and philosophers, men

like Johann Wolfgang von Goethe, for instance, have been fond of walking along this path for relaxation and contemplation. Some say the poets came here to meditate on important things—the burning issues of the day, perhaps, or the meaning of life. Or maybe they had an argument with the wife, I don't know."

I laughed. "Goethe wrote *Faust*, didn't he?"

"Quite so," remarked Dr. Sauer. "Have you read it?"

I shook my head. "But I will if you recommend it."

"I do, I emphatically do," said Dr. Sauer, adding in German, "*Es irrt der Mensch solang er strebt.*"

When he saw my blank look, Dr. Sauer quickly apologized. "Sorry! In English, you would say something like, 'Man errs until he stops striving.'" Then he added, "It's one of the Lord's lines in the play."

It was quiet in the ruins of the monastery. All I could hear was the sound of wind blowing across the mountaintop. There were just a few tourists poking about besides Dr. Sauer and me.

I looked around at the crumbling walls and imagined what the place must have been like when it was an active monastery. By all accounts, the monks had lived simply. Deliberately so. And devoutly—with morning, noon, and evening prayers, regular periods of fasting, and long periods of silence. I wondered how I would have managed living in their community. Would I have had my doubts even then? Perhaps the abbot would have put me to work copying the Bible from ancient Greek to Latin to instill the fear of God in me. Perhaps I would have encountered the peace that eluded me—an epiphany under the stars—on the summit of the Saints' Mountain, unaware of what future conversations it would inspire for those who would traverse its upward path.

Four days later I was back in London and called Mr. Cobb as soon as I found a phone. I couldn't wait to see him and tell him about everything I had seen and learned on my own and from his two friends. Unfortunately, he was out of town and wasn't expected back until the following week.

I felt dejected when I hung up the phone. I had only two days left in London before heading home. I was ready to debrief with Mr. Cobb, even submitting myself to his line of questioning. But it would have to wait. Or perhaps never happen.

I started back to the youth hostel, walking along the Thames. It was a beautiful day. I sat on a bench and looked out at the barges and other boat traffic plying the fabled river. Across the way rose the majestic Houses of Parliament and Big Ben. When the noon hour came, the deep, sonorous chimes of the clock reverberated across the river. I closed my eyes and enjoyed the sun's warmth. The quote from *Faust* replayed in my mind: "Man errs until he stops striving." *But what happens when you no longer strive?*

I thought of the Christians at Kellogg Community College. When I first met them, their "blind" faith had infuriated me, and I had come all this way to prove them wrong. But maybe the bigger picture was that I had come here to finally and fully convince myself that there was, indeed, no meaning or purpose in life, that people throughout history had created religions to relieve their own suffering. Maybe I had come here to explain away not only the world's tragedies of war and famine, but more important, the personal tragedies I had endured—abuse, a broken home, an alcoholic father. I looked at my hands, not realizing I had clenched them into fists.

Sitting beside me on the other end of the bench was an old man feeding pigeons. He didn't look happy as he slowly emptied his brown bag of bread crumbs at his feet. Perhaps he was just concentrating on the job at hand, making sure each of the birds got a little something. Perhaps he was thankful to have found friends who had given him some purpose in life, even if only for a fleeting moment.

Suddenly, I remembered one more library Mr. Cobb said that I needed to visit in London. We had planned to go together but had run out of time. Yes, I still had the address on a slip of paper tucked into my wallet. The Evangelical Library on Chiltern Street near the Baker Street tube station.

I was there in less than twenty minutes. The librarian helped me locate some out-of-print books Mr. Cobb had told me about, and I dutifully began my research. The hours passed slowly.

It was about 6:30 in the evening when I pushed the books to one side and leaned back in my chair. I rubbed my eyes, stared up at the ceiling, and spoke aloud without thinking. "It's true," I said.

I repeated the words. “It’s true.” And a third time, but louder: “It really is true!” This was one time too many for the librarian. She gave me a withering look and I reached for one of the books I had pushed away. But I couldn’t read the words on the page. I felt like a train lurching into the station, letting off a last burst of steam while coming to a final stop. I was speechless. I didn’t know where I was. I only knew I had arrived.

A few minutes later, I was walking down the library steps as dusk gathered over the London streets. I shook my head in disbelief. Mr. Cobb, C. S. Lewis, Dr. Greenleaf, and all the others—they had gotten it right. The Bible was true. I had set out to disprove the Resurrection and discredit Christianity, but there was no escaping the facts. With due respect to Bertrand Russell, he was wrong when he said that people accept Christianity on emotional grounds. For me, the opposite was true. I had been *rejecting* the Christian faith for emotional reasons.

The timing and setting for that moment of epiphany remains a mystery to me to this day. I didn’t fall on my knees and become a Christian on the spot. My eyes may have been opened to the truth, but unlike doubting Thomas, I still resisted responding to it. Even though I knew the truth was irrefutable. I felt ashamed and confused and a failure.

I pondered these things, and much more, on the long trip back to Michigan.

10

New Beginnings

WHEN SCHOOL STARTED in the fall at Kellogg, I made a concerted effort to maintain the image of the carefree Josh McDowell—student leader and perennial party animal of the sophomore class. The first paper I wrote that semester was entitled "How Michigan Can Become Debt Free." My premise called for the state to sell the Upper Peninsula to Wisconsin and legalize prostitution in the capital of Lansing, taxing the proceeds. My statistics showed that the cash from the land sale and the taxable income generated from legalized prostitution would put Michigan in the black. The professor rewarded me with an A!

For all my bluster and bravura, however, I still had to live with myself. I knew my heart was divided, that I was a hypocrite. When I was sure my friends weren't watching,

I would talk with the Christian students about their faith. I made it clear I was only inquiring about things, nothing more, but because I knew more about the subject than many of them, I often had to answer my own questions! On occasion, I even attended church with members of the group. But I held back from making a commitment. I wanted to believe as they believed, but my mind told me to stay away from Christianity like the plague. I had lost my childhood and teen years to what I thought of as divine indifference. I wasn't going to wreck my future over divine interference.

One day I was walking across the commons on a Friday afternoon when I heard my name being called.

"Hey, Josh!"

It was two of my friends, Sam Collins and Dewey Longworth. "What's buzzin', cuzzin? Comin' to the bash tonight?" Sam asked.

"What bash?" I asked.

"Out at the Lake House." replied Sam.

"All the new freshman chicks are gonna be there." gushed Dewey. "You'll have your pick of the litter!"

"Naw, that's all right. I'm going out with someone tonight."

"Well, bring her along too," said Sam. "The more the merrier."

"Just who is this hot babe we've been hearin' about?" chimed in Dewey. "You jacketed or what?"

I looked at my two friends. "Her name is Lynne." Sam

and Dewey waited for me to say more. "Anyway, I gotta split," I said. "I'm late for class."

"Hey, hold on, daddy-o!" said Sam, hurrying after me. "I heard you met this girl at a church. Is that true?"

"Who told you that?"

"That's the word around town, hipster."

"Well, you know what they say."

"What's that?"

"The cutest chicks are the ones that go to church."

"Hey, I wanna go, then!" said Dewey. "What're the show times?"

Sam turned on Dewey. "It's not a movie theater, you kook. Didn't you go to church growin' up?"

"Yeah," said Dewey defensively, "but that was a long time ago."

Sam shook his head. "So where is this church?" he asked as the three of us continued to walk along.

"Factoryville."

Sam and Dewey stopped, giving each other confused looks.

"Factoryville?"

"Where's that?"

"Look it up on the map," I shouted back at them, practically running away.

Factoryville was actually a meandering road in the small town of Athens, located about twenty miles south of Battle Creek. I hadn't exactly lied to Sam and Dewey when I called it a town. In the 1800s there had been a factory of some sort in the area, which gave rise to the town of Factoryville. But that factory had long since disappeared, and the town with it. All that remained was a road and a small country church.

Pastor Logan of Factoryville Bible Church had a peculiar first name: Fay. In his midfifties, he had a warm-hearted, easygoing manner and seemed to take a genuine interest in me.

I really enjoyed his sermons. Armed with all of my research about Christianity, I soon realized Pastor Logan was well-informed and surprisingly intellectual. I wondered why he had decided to pastor what seemed like an insignificant church in the boonies. Since I was far from bashful, I asked him about it one day when the service was over.

He didn't respond immediately. The church had pretty much emptied out and, as usual, I was one of the last to leave. Pastor Logan glanced around the sanctuary, taking it all in. It seemed so peaceful and quaint as the sunlight filtered through the simple windows. "You know, Josh, you'll find a lot of small people in many places around the world," he said, with those kind eyes of his. "Small people doing small things that . . . sometimes . . . change the world." He closed the door to the church, and we walked together down the steps. At that moment, I felt as close to Pastor Logan as I had always hoped I could be with my father, or rather, with the kind of father I wished I had.

But there was another reason I liked going to Factoryville Bible Church.

I met Lynne the first time I attended with some of the Christians from Kellogg Community College. She was sitting at the end of one of the pews, and I noticed her right away. I plopped myself down directly across from her on the other side of the aisle. I knew she would eventually turn and see me. The moment she did, I'd give her the "look"—that certain indefinable, romantic gaze I had refined over many hours in front of the bathroom mirror. As I was preparing myself for the encounter, a man sitting next to Lynne leaned forward and peered sternly at me. From the look he gave me, I could only conclude I was being sized up by Lynne's father.

It turned out to be true. Mr. Merrick was an elder in the church. As I began to spend time with Lynne, he was surprisingly tolerant of me. Maybe it helped that he had two sons who towered over me and told me pointedly how much they loved their younger sister and would do anything to protect her.

I lied to Sam and Dewey, I now reflected, walking into history class and taking a seat. Yeah, I had a new girlfriend named Lynne, but I wasn't going to church with her that Friday evening. She was in Kalamazoo visiting her cousins, and I wouldn't be seeing her the entire weekend. The truth was that I no longer wanted to go to parties where everybody came to get drunk and expected me to be the grand toastmaster.

Most weekends, I preferred being at the Merrick house—not just to hang out with Lynne, but also because

Mrs. Merrick was such an excellent cook. "You can't believe how awful the food is at the school cafeteria," I would complain, passing my plate for a second helping. Mrs. Merrick would smile indulgently, giving me more the second time around than she had the first. I pretended not to see how annoyed Mr. Merrick and his two sons looked as I set to work on the fresh plate of food. Then one of Lynne's sisters would crack a joke and everyone at the table would laugh. It was a big, loving family, and I always enjoyed being with them.

That Sunday, with Lynne still out of town, I skipped the morning service and went in the evening with my friend Larry Minor, who was also a friend of Lynne's sister. We arrived late and decided to sit toward the back. Following the announcements and a hymn, Pastor Logan walked to the pulpit to deliver his sermon. His theme centered on the passage in the Gospel of Luke where the thief on the cross asked Jesus to remember him when He came into His Kingdom. *Why does Pastor Logan keep looking at me?* I wondered. *Or am I only imagining it?*

"Let's be clear," said Pastor Logan midway through. "God's salvation is not an intellectual exercise. In fact, the Bible says God has chosen the foolish things of the world to confound the wise." It seemed he looked directly at me again as he added, "So then, how are we saved?" He turned the pages in his Bible and read Romans 10:9-10: "If thou shalt confess with thy mouth the Lord Jesus, and shalt believe in thine heart that God hath raised him from the dead, thou shalt be saved. For with the heart man believeth unto righteousness; and with the mouth confession is made unto salvation."

Beads of sweat began building on my forehead like small storm clouds. "So tell me, my friend," Pastor Logan continued, "where are you today? Have you confessed Jesus as Lord? Do you believe in His resurrection? And if you do believe, are you ready to commit? Let's review what that commitment will entail . . ."

Pastor Logan spoke a while longer and then invited people to come forward and receive Christ in their heart. I knew I needed to respond, but I couldn't. I stayed glued to my seat. I had heard these invitations before, and all the old fears of losing friends and of committing intellectual suicide pinned me down.

Deep in my heart, I wanted to respond. I wanted to rush down the aisle and do what I should have done in Europe back in the summer. I had discovered the truth there but had balked at accepting its consequences in my life.

Pastor Logan renewed his appeal, quoting Jeremiah 31:3: "Yea, I have loved thee with an everlasting love: therefore with lovingkindness have I drawn thee." He looked up from his Bible and held his arms open. "The Holy Spirit says, 'Come.' He invites you, just as you are. Come to Jesus. Come now."

A seemingly random thought began to run through my mind: *Even if I had been the only person alive the day Jesus died on the cross, He still would have stretched out His arms and died for me.* But why? Why would God do that? Why would He want me? Why would He lavish such love on me when I was still a sinner?

Sensing my anguish, Larry turned to me. "Want me to go up with you?" His question was just the motivation I needed. I was out of my seat in a flash, walking to the altar. I'll never forget the look in Pastor Logan's eyes as I stopped in front of him. His acceptance was full and unconditional as he took my hands in his. I felt like a wayward son returning home. We said a prayer together, and afterward he spent several hours talking to me further about what it meant to be a Christian. This conversation marked the beginning of a long and rewarding discipleship under this wise and devout man.

When I finally left the church later that night, I stopped by my car to breathe in the cool night air. I felt like a man who had been walking in the desert, dying of thirst, and had finally found an oasis. I didn't know what to say or who to thank. I just wanted to drink in the water. I looked up at the moon and smiled, even as warm, salty tears rolled down my face. I asked God again to forgive me for the hardness of my heart, and I felt His presence, His warmth and acceptance, mysteriously and tangibly. My life had been forever changed. I wanted that moment to last forever.

• • •

Winter was long and cold that year, but the fire of a new life in Christ burned steadily within me. I continued my studies at school, and Pastor Logan continued mentoring me in the basics of the Christian faith. When we got to the subject of forgiveness, it became clear that I had business I needed to take care of.

It was just after New Year's when I made the trip to downtown Battle Creek to see Dad at Ritzee's Diner. He was sitting next to the window drinking coffee. He saw me first, I think, because he quickly looked away when I caught sight of him. I had called the meeting, and now I regretted it.

I entered the diner and sat across the table from him and his new girlfriend, Gail. "This is my son Jos," my dad introduced us. She nodded tentatively, extending her hand slowly toward mine. I could only imagine what Dad must have said to her about me.

"What can I get for you, hon?" asked the waitress, appearing from nowhere.

"A cup of coffee, please," I replied.

Dad gestured with his hand. "Get somethin' to eat. My treat."

I shook my head. Coffee would be fine. Dad and I looked at each other for the next several moments. Actually, we each cast furtive glances, then quickly looked somewhere else. Small talk didn't bridge the gap that seemed to stretch interminably between us. *What the heck,* I thought. *I'll just tell him how it is and let him take it or leave it.*

"Dad," I began.

Dad's wiry body tensed up like a dog that knows it's

about to be kicked. "Dad," I repeated, struggling to get the words out. Finally, I unburdened my load. "Dad, I love you."

I don't know who was more surprised—Dad as he heard my words or I as I said them. I absolutely did not want to love my father or forgive him. I was convinced he was responsible for my mother's death and the disintegration of our family. For years, I had gone to bed at night dreaming up ways to kill him without being caught by the police. Even though I was a new Christian, I was still determined to hate him.

The silence was awkward. I looked into my coffee cup as if it held tea leaves and I was trying to read the future. Finally, my father's unsteady voice broke the impasse. "How can you love a father like me?" he asked.

I didn't want to answer him. Not then, anyway. But Pastor Logan had taught me too well. "I'm a Christian now," I said simply. I looked away and so did he. I don't know what he was thinking. Even then, I breathed a silent prayer that God would allow me to keep hating this man who had destroyed his own family. But it wouldn't stick. The hatred continued to slip away. I quickly formed words in my mouth to tell him about all the harm he had caused to the very ones he was called to love and protect. But I knew that if I were to open my mouth again to speak, the same words would come out: *Dad, I love you.*

That's when I knew Christianity was real. I had said

what I had come to say. Not knowing what else to do, I left the diner a short while later.

• • •

Pastor Logan was pleased to hear how the meeting had gone with my father. I was less sure. "Obedience to God's commands," he said, "is not an emotion but an action—a deliberate choice."

"We're called to obey," I added. "The outcome is in God's hands."

"Exactly," said the pastor, smiling. "Which brings us, I feel, to someone else who has figured prominently in your life."

I instantly regretted my statement about obeying God. I could almost smell the man's rancid breath hanging in the air. I got out of my seat and began pacing the floor in Pastor Logan's study. "No way," I said finally. "You can't be serious."

"I'm perfectly serious, Josh."

"It's impossible."

"All things are possible with God."

I looked at Pastor Logan as if he were stabbing me in the back. "You know what he did to me—for years—and who knows how many other boys and young men! How can you ask me to forgive him? I hope he burns in hell! I'll escort him there myself!"

Pastor Logan looked into the fire burning steadily in the fireplace. "Your forgiveness does not condone what he did, Josh. But it does set in motion the process by which you free yourself from the chains of the past. It allows you to move on in life and provides a lost soul with the opportunity for redemption."

Now it was my turn to stare into the fire. "If this is Christianity, maybe I should just hang it up. I understand that in an ideal world forgiveness is the right thing to do. But you're asking too much of me. I cannot forgive Wayne Bailey."

"I'm not asking you to forgive Wayne Bailey, Josh."

"But God is?" I practically spit out the question. *How could God ask me to carry that out?*

Pastor Logan was silent a moment. I looked over at him. He was a good man, but powerless to alter the fundamental course of my life. It was too late for that. I spoke to myself as much as to him: "No one understands. No one."

Pastor Logan looked at me as if he wanted to say something. Instead, he reached for his Bible. He cleared his throat and began to read, "When they came to the place called The Skull, there they crucified Him and the criminals, one on the right and the other on the left. But Jesus was saying, 'Father, forgive them; for they do not know what they are doing.'"

I interrupted his reading. "Wayne Bailey knew exactly what he was doing."

"So did Jesus," replied Pastor Logan.

• • •

It didn't happen immediately; in fact, it took several months and a lot of counseling with Pastor Logan. I remember hoping initially that I wouldn't be able to find out where Wayne lived. But I did find out, and I gave him a call. The conversation was brief. I told him I was coming to see him.

He lived in a drab apartment in Jackson, Michigan. I knocked on the door, he opened it, and I walked inside. He didn't keep his own place as nice as he had kept ours. No teacups or parakeets. I looked at the graying, worn-looking man with troubled eyes and started in without preliminaries. "Wayne, what you did to me was evil. Very evil! But I've come to know Jesus Christ as Savior and Lord. And I've come here . . . to . . . tell you . . ." My carefully rehearsed words failed me. I prayed for strength and realized that what I had to say had to come from my heart, not my head.

I sighed deeply. "Wayne, all of us have sinned, and no one measures up to God's standard of perfection. We all need redemption and, well, I've come here to tell you something you need to hear." He looked at me, his pale eyes unblinking.

For a moment, I wished it weren't true, but it was, and I had to say it out loud. "Christ died for you as much as He did for me. I forgive you, Wayne."

I walked to the door, then faced him a final time. "One other thing, Wayne. Don't let me ever hear of you touching a young man again. You'll regret it."

I walked out to the parking lot and got into my car. *Where is the emotion?* I asked myself, starting up the engine.

Where is the euphoria I should feel having stared down the demon—and the demons—of my past? I pulled out of the parking lot and made my way to the highway nearby. And then it hit me. There was peace in my heart. A peace unlike anything I had experienced before. I had chosen to forgive an enemy out of obedience to God's command, and I had the steady, full peace the Bible describes as surpassing human understanding.

It was a one-hour drive back to Battle Creek. It rained most of the way.

• • •

"I've been thinking, Josh," said Pastor Logan as I walked into his study for my midweek discipleship class.

"Is that so? I thought you were always thinking," I replied.

Pastor Logan smiled and stood up behind his desk. "Why don't we take a walk? It's a beautiful day."

It was late spring, and the Michigan countryside was dense with the rich greens of the trees and the vibrantly colored wildflowers. "I like how Martin Luther put it," said Pastor Logan as we walked down a path through the woods behind his house. "He said that God writes the gospel not just in the Bible, but also on trees, in the flowers, on the clouds and stars." I nodded. I knew this was not what he really had been thinking about and it wasn't what he wanted to talk to me about. Still, I held my peace. "Have you ever heard of Wheaton College?" he continued.

"No," I replied. "Where's that?"

"Outside Chicago. It's where Billy Graham went to school."

"Billy Graham?"

"Yes, Billy Graham. It's a top-notch Christian liberal arts college. I think you should transfer there for your junior and senior years."

"Why?"

"You're ready for the next steps, Josh. I've taken you about as far as I can."

I stopped walking. "Pastor Logan, it's difficult to imagine any college or college professor taking the time and interest in me that you have."

"Be that as it may, Josh, my knowledge and education only extend so far." He continued walking and I fell into step alongside him. "Wheaton is no cakewalk. It will demand a great deal from you academically, but . . ." He turned to look at me with that soft, encouraging smile of his. "I think you're up to the challenge."

"Will it help prepare me for the legal profession?"

"Whatever you decide to do, Wheaton will help you excel. I know some people there, and I'll recommend you highly. If you like, I can make some calls and we'll see what happens."

"Yes, sir, I think that would be great." I breathed in the sweet fragrance of the day, admiring God's gospel in the trees and flowers around me, the billowing clouds and the blue Michigan sky above. *God,* I prayed silently, *if You want me to go to Wheaton, I'm willing.*

11

Wheaton and Beyond

I WAS ACCEPTED as a junior transfer student at Wheaton and entered in the fall of 1960, the college's hundredth anniversary. My course load included economics, history, government, English, and theology. Between studies and my part-time job, it seemed I hardly had time to call Lynne, back in Michigan. But I was happy and expectant about the future.

In January 1961, John F. Kennedy was sworn in as the thirty-fifth president of the United States. In his inaugural address, he called on the nations of the world to fight "the common enemies of man: tyranny, poverty, disease, and war itself." A noble sentiment, and one that I agreed with, but a goal that I knew could not be accomplished apart from the worldwide spread of the gospel of Jesus Christ.

I continued to work hard in school, determined more than ever to be a lawyer. My classes at Wheaton were honing my writing and research skills, my grammar and elocution. Two different Christian businessmen had already approached me with offers to put me through law school—all expenses paid—when I graduated!

The long winter grudgingly gave way to spring. All seemed right with God and the world.

And then the unthinkable happened.

As I listened to the radio in my car at the railroad crossing, the pickup truck slammed into me, spinning my car around and propelling it through the gate. I am sure the train's engineer didn't see what was happening, and even if he did, he would have been powerless to do anything about it.

I'm going to die.

My car stopped less than a foot from the passing train. Another twelve inches and I would have been history. It turned out that the driver of the pickup was drunk.

Upon impact, I had been thrown backward with such force that the steel rods anchoring the front seat to the floor were bent back eight inches. Various witnesses converged on the scene, and after the police arrived and had taken their report, a kindhearted stranger drove me back to my dorm.

As I got out of the car, the man asked me, "Are you sure you're all right?"

At the time, I thought I was just bruised and shaken up, but the next day I collapsed and was rushed to the hospital.

I had suffered severe whiplash. Because my car seat had no headrest, my head had been whipped back over the top of the seat, tearing ligaments in my neck and down my back. The pain was excruciating.

After four days in intensive care, I spent another ten days in the hospital. One morning the doctor informed me I was going to be released and sent home to convalesce. "It's going to be a long process," he said. "You'll be better off at home."

On the surface it seemed reasonable, but I had to wonder if the doctor would have recommended it if he knew what my home life was really like. He must have sensed my unease.

"Your father is going to hire a nurse to look after you."

"You spoke to my dad?"

"I did."

"I thought no one could find him after the accident."

The doctor took a seat beside my bed. "We got in touch with him a few days ago."

I sighed. "How long will I have to be there?"

"I'm thinking three weeks, maybe four. We'll see how it goes."

"But what about my schoolwork? I have exams coming up."

"As far as I know, that's all been taken care of by the administration at the school. Right now, what you have to focus on is getting better. You're going to need a lot of bed rest to do that."

I was still unconvinced. "How am I going to get there?"

"By ambulance."

"Ambulance? All the way to Union City? That's two hundred miles away, doctor."

"You'll be leaving after lunch. You'll be strapped in the back to keep you from moving around." The doctor patted me on the shoulder and I tensed up, literally giving myself a pain in the neck.

"I'm not trying to minimize your situation, son," he continued. "Why don't you try to—I don't know—try to think of the time as sort of a vacation. How does that sound?"

"I'd rather not think about it at all."

If the doctor heard my last comment, he didn't react to it. He had other patients to see and was already halfway out the door. I stared up at the ceiling. Like an epileptic sensing an oncoming seizure, I realized what was about to happen. But I was powerless to stop it. Violent scenes from the past flashed across my mind. I saw my mother's tears and heard her weak protestations. I felt my dad's neck in my hands and remembered ramming his head into the toilet bowl repeatedly, the noise of the flushing water, the strong arms of the police pulling me away, my father spitting water and blood.

I tried to pray. Thankfully, I now knew Jesus was real. He was my friend and comforter. Gradually, I settled down and tried to put things in perspective.

I reminded myself that I had reached a kind of

understanding with my dad. I didn't hate him anymore and even felt remorse for some of the things I had done to him. But it was an uneasy truce at best. I did not want to go home. It was the last place in the world I wanted to be.

12

Going Home

I DIDN'T HAVE an appetite for lunch. One of my Wheaton roommates, Dick Purnell, stopped by the hospital to visit me, and I told him I was going home to recuperate.

"You lucky dog," he said.

"What makes you think I'm so lucky?"

"Home-cooked meals. A familiar bed. Old friends."

"If you put it that way, then yeah, I guess I am lucky." I didn't want Dick or any of my other friends at Wheaton to know what my home life was really like. Just then, two men in black uniforms from the ambulance company came into the room pushing a gurney. Maybe it was the contrast with the dark uniforms, but they struck me as looking extremely pale. One man was tall, the other short, and both had somber expressions. "You guys look like you work for a funeral parlor!" I joked. "Where're you taking me?"

They didn't seem amused and didn't talk much. They transferred me to the gurney, strapped me in, and wheeled me down the hallway as Dick waved good-bye. "See you soon, Josh," he said. "We're all praying for you, buddy!"

I wanted to raise my arm to give Dick a farewell wave, but I couldn't move any part of my body. The lights in the ceiling blurred past me as the two attendants wheeled me through the emergency room and outside to the waiting ambulance. It was a big, smooth-riding Cadillac, painted orange and white.

The shorter attendant took a seat in the back of the ambulance with me.

"I'm Gunther," he said.

I noticed he was short of breath.

"Are you okay?" I asked, ready to trade places and let him lie down on the gurney.

"Heart condition," he said matter-of-factly.

"What exactly's the problem?" I asked.

"My ticker don't pump blood the way it should. The docs give it a fancy name but I call it pulseless disease."

"As in no pulse?"

Gunther nodded and held out his wrists. "No pulse here." He lifted his leg a little. "No pulse there."

"You're a living miracle, Gunther," I said.

Gunther recited his litany of ailments. "Can't see outta my left eye and I see white spots outta my right eye. I get dizzy, too. Faintin' spells . . . headaches . . ."

"And yet none of those things seem to get in the way of you doing your job."

Gunther pursed his lips. "I've been given up for dead three times. But I keep snapping back."

"I guess it helps to work for an ambulance company. Just in case."

Gunther laughed. That was a good sign. It was going to be a long ride.

• • •

I must have dozed off for a few hours.

"We're almost there," said Gunther. "We're passing through Union City now."

The ambulance had long windows on both sides of the rear compartment where Gunther and I were, and I could turn my eyes enough to make out bits and pieces of the small town's landmarks. The building for the *Register Tribune*. Hensley's 5 & 10. Whiting's Drug Store and Fabiano's Ice Cream Parlor along Broadway. The commercial dairy where local farmers sold their milk. The feed store. The infamous Duffy's Tavern.

I glimpsed the sun reflecting off the St. Joe River and knew we were about four miles away from the farm. When we turned onto the lane leading to the farmhouse, it was as if every bump and rut had turned out to greet me. I felt like the guy with sunburn who keeps getting slapped on the back by his friends.

For a fleeting moment, the big willow tree next to the house came into view, with its green branches swaying in the breeze like beaded curtains. At least that was one good memory of home. Just knowing it would be nearby brought an unexpected sense of comfort.

The ambulance came to a stop and then backed up to the front porch of the house. As it turned out, there was no nurse to greet me. *Big surprise,* I thought to myself. *I wonder if Dad remembered to show up.* Just then, I could smell my father's cigarette smoke and heard him directing the two attendants where to take me. As we entered the house, I could hear Gunther breathing hard.

"You all right, Gunther?" I asked him.

Gunther set down his side of the gurney. "Maybe I could just catch a few."

"What's the matter?" I heard my dad asking him.

"He doesn't have a pulse," I said.

"Doesn't have a pulse!"

"I haven't dropped anyone yet," said Gunther, shakily picking up his side of the gurney again.

Dad had moved the furniture out of the living room and put in a bed to make things easier on everyone. I winced as Gunther and the ambulance driver helped me from the gurney into the bed and strapped me in. As I stared up at the ceiling, I could hear Dad outside, thanking them for their help. After a while, I heard the ambulance leave, and then I sensed my dad standing in the room.

"What happened to the nurse?" I asked.

"She couldn't make it today. She'll be here tomorrow."

I grew quiet. There was something different in my dad's voice. As he talked, I realized what it was—he was sober.

"Can I get you anything?" he asked.

"Nothing for now."

I heard Dad's footsteps as he walked into the adjoining family room and sat down in his favorite chair. It grew eerily quiet in the house. Then I heard Dad striking a match to light up another cigarette. A fly began buzzing about the room. It seemed unnaturally loud. I began to follow its erratic movements and thought about what the doctor had said just before he sent me home: "Think of this as a vacation." Right. I should have asked him to hypnotize me before the ambulance took me away.

I'm not sure how much time passed or if I drifted off to sleep. I suddenly became aware of someone else in the room with me, someone watching me quietly. But I couldn't lift my head to look around.

"Dad?" I called. "Are you there?" I heard a sniffling sound. Instinctively, I tried to sit up for a better look. The pain was excruciating, and I fell back on the pillow. I strained my eyes to see as best I could whoever was in the room. Then I saw him out of the corner of my eye, standing near the window. He looked bent over, as if his stomach hurt. Dad.

"Why are you crying?" I asked him.

He didn't answer. Instead, he began to pace back and forth. *Maybe he's going through withdrawal pains,* I reasoned, still marveling that he seemed sober. I knew he had been attending AA meetings regularly. Maybe the program was working for him. *But what if something happens to him?* I wondered. *What will I do? I can barely move my head off the pillow.*

Suddenly, Dad sat on the edge of the bed next to me. "Dad, what's wrong?" I asked. I had never seen him like this. The tears in his eyes scared me.

Finally, he spoke in a faltering voice. "How . . . can you . . . ever . . ." Then he grew silent again. I thought he was going to stand up and walk away when he suddenly finished the sentence. "How can you . . . ever . . . love a father . . . like me?"

I was speechless.

He sat awhile looking down at me, then gazed out the window as he wiped the tears from his eyes. "That day in the diner . . . the day you said . . . you loved me."

"Yes, Dad."

He started to cry again. "How?"

I didn't know what to say. Thoughts raced through my mind, but I couldn't find the words. He stood up and began to pace again. "Dad," I said finally. "Dad . . ."

He stopped pacing. I could hear the curtains fluttering in the open window, then felt him sit on the bed again. When I looked up, I couldn't believe what I was seeing. He had never shown much love to anyone—certainly not to me. But now he appeared to be on the verge of falling apart.

"Dad," I said again, then paused. "I've learned one thing that has completely changed my life. God became man, and His name is Jesus. And Dad, Jesus is passionate about having a relationship with you."

Dad fixed his eyes on me again and searched my face wonderingly. I wished I were a mind reader. *What is he thinking?* It seemed as if time had come to a standstill. Then he stood and walked out of the house.

I'm not sure how much time passed. It was warm and the fly was still buzzing around. Perhaps forty-five minutes went by before Dad came back in. He leaned over me and I could see fresh tears on his face. *Why on earth is he still crying?*

"Jos," he said, "if Jesus can do for me what I've seen Him do in your life, then I want to know Him."

Now it was my turn to cry. "You need to ask Him into your life, Dad. You need to open your heart to Him and pray."

"I don't reckon I know how to pray, son."

"Just tell Him what's in your heart."

Dad nodded and said a simple, down-to-earth prayer, a "farmer's prayer," if you will. "God, if You are God, and if Christ is Your Son . . . and if You can forgive me for what I've done to my family . . ." His voice broke. He composed himself and sighing deeply, prayed the heartrending words, "And if You can do in my life what I've seen You do in my son's life, then please . . ." Dad struck his chest and cried out, "Please come in!"

Dad was hunched over sobbing, clearly broken. I was crying too; as the tears welled up in my eyes, everything became blurry, like I was underwater, looking up from the bottom of a swimming pool. I could feel the tears wetting my face but had to let them go because I couldn't move. Then I felt a gentle touch on my face, the sweetest gesture you can imagine. Dad wiped my tears away. The intense joy in my heart made me cry even more.

You know, when a person gives his or her life to Christ, everything changes. When I made that commitment, my attitude and actions began to change over a period of a year and a half. But when my father came to Christ, the transformation was immediate. He changed right in front of me! It was as if someone reached down inside him and turned on a switch that flooded light into a dark room.

The rest of the day passed quietly as Dad and I talked off and on into the night. When it was time for bed, I asked Dad to leave the window open. I wanted to hear the sound of the train in the distance.

• • •

Nurse Gibbs showed up the following day. She was efficient, if humorless. I had to wonder how things would have played out if she had arrived the day before, as scheduled. Would Dad have been so emotional and transparent? Would he have spent time with me? Would he have prayed? I doubt it. Only God knows, of course, but the Bible says to give thanks in every situation, and considering how things worked out, I needed to give God thanks for the accident at Wheaton that nearly took my life.

I convalesced at home for three weeks. Most evenings after Nurse Gibbs had left for the day, Dad would come and sit in a chair near my bed. Summer was approaching and the days were growing longer. Dad was quietly attentive to my needs. He asked me questions about how to live a Christian life and how to please God. He wanted to make up for lost time.

I had brought my Bible with me, and since Dad didn't know the Scriptures at all, I was able to direct him to several key passages. He wasn't the greatest of readers, but he understood the words, and often a profound silence would linger in the room after he had read a particular verse that hit home for him.

"Verily, verily, I say unto you," he read slowly one evening from the Gospel of John. "He that heareth my word, and believeth on him that sent me, hath everlasting life, and shall not come into condemnation; but is passed from death unto life."

"Believe in Jesus, Dad. Believe in God," I encouraged him. "Read His Word and put it into practice." That's how we would spend our evenings together—reading the Bible and discussing what we read.

One evening Dad was agitated when he entered the room. Finally, it came out. He had a confession to make. "Son, I'm an alcoholic, and I know I'm an alcoholic. I joined AA to try to break the habit, but I've always known I'll have to be on guard against it all my life." He looked at me to see if I had anything to say, but I was quiet. "Well, earlier today out in the barn I was shoveling some manure when the urge came over me to take another drink. I don't know where the thought came from, where the desire came from, because it was so sudden and so strong. And I remembered where I had hidden a bottle—near half-full it was. And I went and took it out and uncorked it and took a good swig."

I'm sure Dad saw the disappointment on my face, because his next words were said with great conviction. "But son, I still don't know what happened. It was like I had put poison on my tongue or it had caught on fire. I couldn't swallow the wine. I just spit it out and poured the bottle out on the floor."

I tried to sit up in bed, but it hurt too much. "Dad, that's the best news I've heard in a long time!" I exclaimed. "Don't you see how Jesus Christ has changed your life from the inside out?"

"I reckon He has, son. I reckon He has."

At his next AA meeting, Dad shared his story. He couldn't wait to tell me what the reaction was.

"They cheered and applauded me!" he said excitedly. When someone there asked Dad how he had managed to exercise such self-control, he told them about opening his heart to Jesus. He had even quoted a verse from the Bible: "Come unto me, all ye that labour and are heavy laden, and I will give you rest."

"Dad," I said, interrupting, "I never thought I'd say this, but I sure am proud of you. I only wish Mom could have been here to see how you've changed."

Dad nodded. "The group wants me to go with them to the state pen in Jackson in two weeks."

"The penitentiary? To tell your story?"

Dad smiled and touched my shoulder. "They do." I suddenly remembered Wayne Bailey touching my shoulder. As a boy I had cried forlornly for my dad's embrace . . . for any sign of affection from him. A love that never came—until now.

• • •

As the time neared for me to return to Wheaton, Pastor Logan called. "How're you getting back to Wheaton?" he asked me.

"I guess I'll take the bus," I said.

"No, no. I'll take you back," my friend and mentor insisted.

"That's a long drive, sir," I said.

"With good company," he remarked.

I couldn't have been happier. I had called Pastor Logan when my dad accepted Christ, and he was thrilled at the news. I wanted the two of them to meet, but I didn't know how I was going to pull it off because I had been unable to attend church since the accident. Now I'd be able to introduce them to each other before leaving for Wheaton. Everything was coming together.

A few days later, Larry Minor and some friends from Battle Creek picked me up for a relaxing day in Benton Harbor on Lake Michigan. Nurse Gibbs had insisted that I wear my neck brace since it was my first time outside the house. Once we got to the beach, we started playing volleyball. Within a few seconds, I knew I was in trouble—the pain was more than I could bear. I had to sit down, feeling like a crippled old man. Even though I was sad about my limitations, I had much to be thankful for. "The vanity of youth!" I shouted at my friends, watching them play hard and dive into the sand for a loose ball.

The blue water of the lake sparkled in the sunlight. I closed my eyes and prayed, thanking God for big and little things—for my father's salvation, for the warmth of the sun on my back. I would be back at school in three more days, hurling myself into the flurry of term papers and final exams. For the moment, I didn't want to think about all the catching up I had to do.

• • •

I was up early the day I left home. I heard Pastor Logan's car coming up the lane. Dad opened the screen door and stepped outside, carrying my small bag.

"Hello, Mr. McDowell," said Pastor Logan, getting out of his car and walking up the steps to the front porch. The two men shook hands. "It's a pleasure meeting you. I've heard a lot about you."

Dad averted his eyes. "Not much good, I'm afraid."

"Not at all, sir. Not at all."

I stepped outside. "Dad, I see you've met my spiritual father, Pastor Logan."

Dad nodded. "So, Jos, does that make me your spiritual

son?" he asked with a twinkle in his eye. Then he smiled at Pastor Logan. "And you must be my grandfather."

Pastor Logan laughed and put his arms around the two of us. "We're all God's children," he said as we walked together to the car.

"I hope you'll come and visit us at church sometime," said Pastor Logan to my dad.

"I just might," said Dad. "I do stay pretty busy with my AA meetings, though."

"And that's a great thing," I chimed in. "Just don't forget that the Divine Power you talk about at AA is just another name for Jesus Christ." I caught a warning look from Pastor Logan and changed the subject. "Anyway, the church is on Factoryville Road in Athens. You can't miss it."

Dad opened the car door for me and helped me inside. "It's been good having you here, son."

"Hey, Dad, I left my Bible for you on the nightstand. Will you read it every day?"

"I will."

"And pray for me?"

"I will."

"I'll be praying for you too, Dad." As Pastor Logan started the car, I took a long look at my father. "I love you, Dad."

Dad squeezed my arm. "I love you, too, son."

"When I come back in the summer, we'll go fishing!"

"I'd like that very much."

"Count it done!" I shouted.

As we drove off, I angled the rearview mirror to catch a final glance of Dad. I could see him on the steps of the porch, watching and waving, until we turned the corner and he disappeared from view.

Pastor Logan and I talked nonstop during the trip to Illinois. Not only did we lose track of the time, Pastor Logan evidently lost track of the speedometer. A police siren grew louder behind us, and soon we were being pulled over.

"Good morning, sir," said the policeman when Pastor Logan rolled down his window. "Can I see your driver's license, please?"

Pastor Logan handed it to the policeman. "What's the problem, officer?" he asked.

The policeman looked over Pastor Logan's license, speaking absentmindedly. "Speeding in a school zone. There was a sign behind you."

"I didn't see it," said Pastor Logan.

"It's there."

"I'm very sorry. Just what does it say?"

"'Speed Limit 25 When Children Are Present,'" remarked the policeman writing out a ticket and handing it to Pastor Logan. "You were doing thirty-five. You'll need to go to the courthouse and pay the fine."

"Or contest the fine," I remarked.

The policeman leaned down to get a better look at me. "There's nothing to contest, young man. It's an open-and-shut case."

"See you in court," I said calmly. Pastor Logan gave me a horrified look.

"What are you doing?" he mouthed at me.

I just smiled back.

"Alrighty then, follow me," said the policeman, heading back to his cruiser.

Pastor Logan was embarrassed by the entire incident, ready and more than willing to pay the fine. I had other ideas.

My defense was simple and straightforward. "Your Honor, the sign said 'Speed Limit 25 When Children Are Present,' but in fact, there was only *one* child present in the neighborhood when we were driving by."

The judge looked up from his desk and squinted at me. "What is that again?"

"The sign, Your Honor . . . The sign warning motorists to slow down is very clear: 'When *Children* Are Present.' In other words, more than one child. However, as I stated previously, there was only one child present at the time of the alleged infraction. So you see, Your Honor, the good pastor was not disobeying the law as represented by the sign."

The judge looked at me awhile, then looked over at Pastor Logan, and finally looked at the policeman who had booked us. "How long have I been a judge here?"

"I'm not sure, Your Honor. Several years before I joined the force."

"Son," the judge said, peering back at me, "I don't know how sound your legal reasoning is, but I have to hand it to you. That's the most unusual defense I've heard in all the years I've been a judge here in LaPorte County. Case dismissed."

Outside the courthouse, Pastor Logan gave me a big hug. "*That* is why you're going into law!"

I stood a little taller as I walked over to Pastor Logan's car, nodding at the policeman before getting inside. When we arrived in Wheaton, Pastor Logan bought me lunch at the Seven Dwarfs Restaurant, and when we finished the meal, I ordered a banana split for dessert. Dick Purnell and Frank Kifer were waiting at the house we shared near campus and helped me get settled. There was one more month of classes to go. I worked hard and did well on all my final exams.

With school wrapped up for another year, I called Dad and told him to get the fishing poles ready.

13

Summer 1961

THE FIRST WEEK back home, Dad and I went to McRae's Restaurant in town for breakfast. I never passed up a free meal, and McRae's was well known for its down-home cooking. I was ready to attack a big stack of pancakes when a familiar voice behind me greeted my dad. "Hello, Wilmot. Good to see you this morning."

It was Mr. Austin, one of Dad's friends, standing nearby. He owned an auto repair shop on St. Joseph Street.

"Mind if I have a seat?" asked Mr. Austin.

"Sure thing," said Dad, scooting over in the booth. "You remember Jos."

"Of course I do," said Mr. Austin, extending his hand across the table. "You home for the summer?"

"Yes sir. Just finished my junior year."

"Well, that's a good thing, I guess," said Mr. Austin. "He workin' for you, Wilmot?"

"Don't need to. Not much goin' on at the farm anymore. Shorty pretty much runs the place now."

"That's what I heard." Then he turned back to me. "Need a job, son? I'm lookin' for a good mechanic."

"Thank you, Mr. Austin, but I have my own company to run."

"Is that so?"

"Superior Painting Company," said Dad. "He's got a whole raft of people workin' for him. Mostly fast-talkin' college kids."

I couldn't miss Mr. Austin's smirk. "I don't know if I'd want a buncha college kids workin' for me."

"Why's that?" I asked.

"Smart alecks. Think they know everything."

"But you just offered *me* a job, Mr. Austin."

"See what I mean?" said Mr. Austin, gesturing to Dad. "Smart alecks!"

The three of us laughed as the waitress walked up to our table. She handed Mr. Austin a menu. "Coffee, Mr. Austin?"

"You bet," he said, turning over his coffee cup for the waitress to fill. "You're lookin' good, Wilmot. Real good. Where's your lady friend?"

Dad glanced at me quickly. "She's in Tacoma. But she'll be comin' here first part of July."

"Who's that, Dad?" I asked.

"Berta. Berta Simpkins. I'll tell you more about her later."

"Please do."

Mr. Austin stirred his coffee. "We don't see you anymore over at Duffy's."

"I got better things to do, Frank."

"So I hear."

"And you know what else?" continued Dad.

"I've heard about that too," said Mr. Austin peremptorily.

"How long we known each other, Frank?"

Mr. Austin took a sip of coffee. "It's got to be more than twenty years, I s'pose. I remember when this one here was born," he said, nodding at me. "You passed out cigars that night at Duffy's."

"You passed out cigars when I was born?"

"Hav-a-Tampas," said Mr. Austin before my dad could say anything. "And you bought three or four rounds for everybody too."

"I reckon I did," said Dad. "But I tell you what, Frank, if I could give you anything now, it'd be Jesus. He's changed my life completely. Thanks to my son here."

Mr. Austin looked across at me. "So you're to blame."

"He ain't to blame," said Dad before I could speak. "Thank God he found the Lord when he did. Otherwise, I'd still be stumblin' round town drunk as a skunk."

"I was just kiddin', Wilmot," said Mr. Austin. "Everyone in town knows you're a changed man. For the better, they say."

"Well, what do you think, Frank? I'm right here beside you. Am I a changed man?"

Mr. Austin sipped his coffee. He wasn't going to answer the question. But Dad was not dissuaded. "What the Lord did for me, Frank, He can do for you, too. God don't play favorites, ya know. He loves us all the same. He died on that cross for you just like He did for me." Dad grew silent as their eyes met. "Why don't you come to Him now, Frank?"

Mr. Austin's face reddened. "Here?"

"Why not? Good a place as any."

"What do you mean 'come to Him' anyway?"

"Give your life to Him. Give Him the keys to your heart. Fall in love with Him."

"Good God, Wilmot! Save it for church."

"If I save it for church, Frank, I might never get another chance to tell you 'bout it."

"What can I get you, Mr. Austin?" The waitress suddenly reappeared at our table, ready to take his order. Mr. Austin glanced quickly at the menu.

"Give me whatever he's eating," said Mr. Austin. "And bring me the check, too. For the three of us."

"You don't need to do that," Dad protested mildly.

"I feel like doin' it," said Mr. Austin. "Is that okay with you?"

"It's fine with me," I chimed in.

Frank Austin didn't pray to receive Christ that morning, but he seemed to listen carefully as Dad explained the gospel message. When it was time to go, more people stopped us on the way out, all of them eager to speak with Dad or just say hello. Word spreads fast in a small town, and the word was out—Wilmot McDowell was a different man.

I couldn't ever remember a previous time in my life when I had wanted to be seen with Dad in public. It was humiliating to be related to the town drunk. On several occasions, Mom had forced me to go into town to try to find him and bring him home. Once I discovered him passed out on a street corner, just like one of the derelicts I had seen in the Chicago slums, those times when a group of us from Wheaton went into the city to help out at various homeless shelters. Now for the first time ever, I couldn't have been prouder to be Wilmot McDowell's son. He was making a difference in Union City. People were changing for the better because of the changes they saw in him! And from everything I heard, he was having the same impact in the prisons he visited, talking about his new life in Christ.

As we stepped out of McRae's into the bright sunlight along Broadway, I was reminded of Mr. Cobb's words about the power of personal testimony and how the changed lives of Jesus' followers became, perhaps, the greatest witness of all that Jesus was Lord of lords and King of kings. My dad had become a disciple of Jesus Christ! Who would have believed it?

I suddenly blurted out, "Dad, I love you. No conditions. No reservations."

Dad stood there, taking my words in. "I love you, too, son," he said finally.

We started down the sidewalk toward my car. "Tell me about Berta," I said.

"Berta?"

"Your lady friend. Am I the last one to know what's goin' on?"

"Berta Simpkins," said Dad. "We're gonna get married next month."

"What?" I couldn't get my response out fast enough.

"What's that?" Obviously Dad didn't hear me.

"You're getting married?"

"Sure am," said Dad smiling. "How about them apples?"

I didn't answer. I think it was the smile on his face more than anything else that ticked me off. Getting married? I wanted to be happy for him, but I was conflicted. *Has he completely forgotten about Mom, how he robbed her of a love-filled marriage? After all he's done, he dares to . . .* I didn't finish the thought.

We drove home in silence. Dad knew better than to push things. I dropped him off and headed to Athens, where I had a crew painting a house. *Unconditional love*, I repeated in my mind, driving down the highway. *No reservations.* It had been less than an hour since I said those words in complete sincerity to my dad on the sidewalk in front of McRae's. Now here I was, being tested and failing big time.

"I am crucified with Christ," the apostle Paul had written. "Nevertheless I live; yet not I, but Christ liveth in me."

I was living and breathing all right, but where was Jesus? When would I die on that cross and let the Lord have His way? I couldn't answer my own questions.

That Sunday I invited Dad to Factoryville Bible Church. After the service, I introduced him to Lynne and her family.

"Are you going to marry my son?" Dad had a knack for speaking his mind.

"Dad!" I protested.

"What? She's darn good lookin' and she goes to church, too! What more do you want?"

"Actually," said Lynne, showing a lot of composure, "I think your son is one of the nicest young men I know. I'm proud to be his girlfriend."

"There!" exclaimed Dad, feeling justified. "You see that? She's proposin' to you."

"Will you excuse us?" I said to Lynne and her family, hurrying Dad out of the church.

"Where're we goin', son?" asked Dad as I hauled him away.

"A Sunday afternoon drive," I said curtly.

"Wonderful! It's a beautiful day."

It *was* a beautiful day. The trees and fields were a lush green and the sun's rays seemed to be shooting holes through the billowing clouds. I turned on the car radio and settled back in the driver's seat. "There's someplace I'd like to see, Dad."

"Sure, where's that?"

"Where Mom is buried. Do you mind?"

"Why should I mind?"

"So where is she buried?" I asked.

"You don't know?"

I shook my head. "I don't remember, Dad. When I got that blow to the head in the Air Force, my memory was affected. I had amnesia for a while."

"I didn't know that."

"I told you before," I said, getting defensive.

"I guess I had amnesia too," said Dad quietly, "but for different reasons."

"There are still things I can't remember from around that time," I continued. "I don't remember Mom's funeral at all. Nothing."

"Turn left up ahead," Dad directed.

Fifteen minutes later, we pulled into Riverside Cemetery and parked the car. Dad led me to a simple gravestone with Mom's name on it. There were no flowers on the grave, and the weeds had grown up around it. We stood silently, listening to the songbirds and enjoying the summer breeze blowing through the flowering dogwood and Juneberry.

"I should come here more often," said Dad.

"Why?" I asked.

Dad didn't answer my question. "When I go, I want you to put me here with your mom," he said, bending down to pull up some weeds.

"What about Berta?"

"She'll understand," he said simply.

I helped Dad clear the grave of weeds. A week later, we

came again and put a bouquet of flowers next to Mom's headstone.

• • •

Berta came to town as planned, and after spending time with her, I began to see her in a different light. She was a sweet-natured woman and good to my dad, as well as good for him. But after they got married, it was hard for me to be around her much. As much as I tried not to let it bother me, I was disturbed that she was the beneficiary of the positive changes in my dad's life. She got to experience the "new Wilmot." Mom had only known the drunken, abusive one.

One warm evening in August, a few days before my birthday, I was sitting alone on the front porch when Dad came out. "Mind if I sit awhile?"

"It's your house, Dad."

"Not for long, son," he said, settling into his favorite rocker.

"What do you mean?"

"When I'm gone, this house will belong to you children."

"I'm sure you'll be around for a long time, Dad. Your children won't want this house."

"You're right. Nobody much comes around now."

"Yeah, well, I wish they would," I said, trying to be upbeat. "They should experience the new you. By the way, what do you hear about Junior?"

"Junior? He's out in East Lansing."

That didn't surprise me. After Junior had moved his wife and "house," we had pretty much cut all family ties. Last I'd heard, he had moved to East Lansing to attend Michigan State University. No doubt he had put down roots there. I'd heard he had done well financially.

"Dad, there's somethin' I've been wantin' to ask you."

"Shoot."

"That dispute you had with Junior up on the hill . . ."

"I don't remember much about that."

"But you remember that it happened."

"Somewhat."

"Dad, did you give Junior half the farm?"

Dad rocked a few seconds before answering. "You have to understand that Junior worked for eight years without any pay . . ."

"But you did eventually give him half the dollar value of the farm, didn't you?" I interrupted.

"Jos, if it hadn't been for Junior, we'd likely have lost everything. You know how I was back then."

"Oh, I remember very well." Something told me to drop the subject, but I couldn't. "And you also paid Junior's tuition at Michigan State. Isn't that true?"

Dad nodded. "We paid for your sister June's, too."

"But when it came time for me to go to college, you couldn't help."

"When it come time for you to go to college, son, I was pretty much broke. Nuthin' left."

"Oh, there was something left," I said, staring off in the dark.

"Hardly nuthin', Jos."

"Not even enough to pay the light bill?" I asked, referring to the response he gave me that first year at Kellogg when I wanted to live at home to save money.

Dad stopped rocking and lowered his head."I'm sorry about that, Jos. That was wrong of me. I hope you can forgive me."

I didn't reply, trying to calm down before I said something I'd regret. The sounds of the crickets and the television playing softly inside the house filled the silence. Dad began to rock again.

"What does Junior do now?" I asked.

"He sells insurance," said Dad.

"Insurance? I thought he had studied agriculture."

"He did. But somewhere along the way he took up sellin' insurance. He's gotten pretty good at it from what I hear. Someone told me that he's rewritten one of the state manuals. I don't know much about it."

Why should I be surprised? Junior was good at everything he did.

"But last I heard," continued Dad, "he was planning on joinin' the Peace Corps."

"What?"

"Goin' over to Africa with Carla and Julie."

"I don't believe it."

"Well, it's true."

"I still don't believe it."

"Maybe you should go over and see him 'fore you head back to college."

Dad's rocker grew quiet and he spoke softly, almost gently. "You know, son, if I could, I'd do a lotta things different. I know it's too late now to change things, but if I could, I would. I just want you to know that."

I sighed and looked out at the sky. The moon was behind a band of slow-moving clouds, illuminating them to a glistening silver. What right did I have to hold a grudge against Dad?

"What would you change?" I asked.

Dad's rocker started to creak again, and the seconds ticked by. I heard him clearing his throat and looked over at him, realizing he was trying to speak. The moonlight picked up the glint of tears in his eyes. Inside the house, Berta called him. Neither of us said anything, knowing she'd find us soon enough.

"There you are," she said cheerily, opening the screen door and stepping onto the porch. "I was wonderin' where you'd made off to."

"Hi, Bertie," said Dad, clearing his throat.

"Have a seat," I said, standing.

"No, Jos. You don't need to do that."

"No, no. Go ahead." I looked over at Dad. "I was thinkin' I need to go into Battle Creek tomorrow. Maybe the three of us could catch a movie downtown."

"Really?" asked Berta, sitting down next to Dad. "How nice. I'd love to! Is that all right with you, Wilmot?"

"Sure."

The following afternoon we caught the matinee of *Voyage to the Bottom of the Sea* at the Bijou Theatre on West Michigan Avenue. Near the end of the film, when Joan Fontaine fell into a shark tank and was killed, Berta grabbed my hand and held it for the rest of the movie.

• • •

My birthday was August 17, and Dad and I celebrated by going fishing at the lake behind Mr. Berger's farm. (His farm was across the road from us.) We stayed out well after dark. Not that the fish were biting much or that Dad and I had important things to talk about or that we were trying to solve the world's problems, but all my life I had wanted to go fishing with him. Finally the dream was coming true.

The next day was Friday, and when I finished work, we drove into town and rented a small boat to fish for bullhead out on the St. Joe River. We brought home a good catch, and I have to compliment Berta—the way she prepared that fish was mouthwatering.

As for my relationship with Lynne, things got more serious. I realized that marriage was imminent—still a ways out, mind you, but visible on the horizon. To be honest, thinking about it made me nervous. I kept hearing those words that began the old radio drama *The Shadow*: "Who knows what evil lurks in the hearts of men?" Who knows, indeed? The prophet Jeremiah had said something similar in the Bible: "The heart is deceitful above all things, and desperately wicked: who can know it?"

I couldn't shake the questions that kept nagging me. *How free am I of the past? Will I bring old wounds and old baggage into a marriage relationship with Lynne? How can I prevent the past from tainting the future?*

I went to see Pastor Logan.

"It seems we've had this conversation before, Josh," said the pastor, settling back in his chair.

"I've never talked to you about this before, pastor."

"No, but that's not what I mean." Pastor Logan took a notepad and sketched two intersecting lines on a piece of paper. "What do you see?" he asked me.

"A cross."

"And Jesus said what? 'Take up your cross daily . . .'"

"'. . . and follow me,'" I finished the sentence.

"Correct." Pastor Logan traced the vertical line of the cross. "Think of this part of the cross as your relationship with God," he said. "Up and down. You on earth and God in heaven."

"Okay."

Then Pastor Logan drew over the horizontal line. "In this direction, you have your relationship with your fellow man, your neighbor. That includes all humanity, even those who have sinned against you, as you discovered when you went to see Wayne. So what does this mean? The cross goes both ways, you see. We can't have one without the other.

We can't have peace with God and not have peace with our fellow man."

"I'm sorry, pastor, but I don't get it," I said impatiently. "Lynne is my girlfriend. I don't hold anything against her at all. If anything, she's too good for me!"

Pastor Logan sighed. "I wasn't thinking of Lynne."

"Who, then? My dad? We're workin' things out—kind of . . ."

"You tell me, Josh. I'm not a mind reader. Better yet, allow the Holy Spirit to search your heart and speak to you."

I looked at the floor, knowing what the problem was. At least on the surface. I still harbored resentment toward my brother, Junior, but was too proud to admit it. As to what else might be lurking in the recesses of my heart—well, only God knew. "Search me, O God, and know my heart," I heard Pastor Logan saying. "Try me, and know my thoughts."

"Is your answer to always read me something from the Bible?" I asked sharply, eyes flashing, before I realized he wasn't reading the Bible. He was leaning forward in his chair, eyes shut, praying. "See if there be any wicked way in me," he continued, "and lead me in the way everlasting. Amen."

"You're right, pastor," I said quietly, after a long silence. "We have had this conversation before."

Pastor Logan stood up and walked over to his office window. It had started to rain, and the raindrops were pattering against the glass. "You need the guidance of the

Holy Spirit, Josh. We all do." He paused, then went on. "We don't reach the finish line the day we start the race. We struggle every day to be more like Christ. All of us do. But we're called to endure for the sake of the glory yet to come." He turned to look at me. "The Christian life is not a sprint, son. It's a marathon. Be filled with the Spirit and pace yourself. There's much more to come."

After talking with Pastor Logan, I decided to remedy one thing that was bothering me—I'd write Junior a letter. I wanted to clear the air and tell him how I felt about things, thinking that was a way of reconciling with him. However, every time I sat down to write, I always ended up throwing the letter away before I was finished. Finally, I decided a postcard would suffice. I went to Hensley's 5 & 10 and bought him a nice touristy one with a picture of the Mackinac Bridge suspended over the blue waters of the Straits of Mackinac.

Junior,

I forgive you for what you did to the family, and to Mom and Dad, but I never want to see you again.

That's as good as I can do, I said to myself. *At least I'm being honest.* I got Junior's address from Dad and put the card in the mail, even though I knew deep down I was going about this the wrong way. It was as if Pastor Logan had never even spoken to or prayed for me about what I needed to do.

Finally, my conscience got the better of me. As the time approached for me to return to Wheaton, I decided to leave a few days early and see if I could visit Junior. The night before I left, I phoned him.

"It's me. Jos."

"Jos?" said Junior. I could hear the shock in his voice. "Where are you?"

"Down on the farm with Dad. I thought I'd come by and see you."

"Well, sure. I guess so . . ."

"I'm on my way back to school. You probably didn't know I was going to college."

"Kellogg Community?"

"No, I'm goin' to Wheaton. I'm a senior."

"Wheaton College, over by Chicago?"

"Yeah."

"Coming up here is out of your way, isn't it?"

"Yeah. Yeah, I guess it is. But, well . . ." I almost hung up the phone before Junior interjected.

"You're welcome to come if you like."

I hesitated. "Did you get my card?"

"Yes. Pretty photograph."

"Well, look, I gotta tell you, I'm so embarrassed I sent that card. I don't know what got into me. It was really stupid of me to do that, and I'd like to apologize."

"It's okay, Jos. When do you want to come by?"

"Tomorrow afternoon, if that's okay."

"You bet," said Junior. "I'll let Carla know."

I slept soundly that night, though I had a strange dream of being in a large, dark room looking for a bird that was chirping. I finally found it, inside a cage on the floor. I opened the door of the cage and the bird flew away.

• • •

It's about seventy miles north from Union City to East Lansing. I got there earlier than expected, but everyone was home—Junior and Carla and their nine-year-old daughter, Julie. Junior looked the same as I remembered him, though he had put on a few pounds. It was strange seeing him after so many years.

"Look at you, little brother," he said, grinning and shaking my hand. "You've grown up on me!"

"It's good to see everybody," I said. "Hello, Carla. How are you?"

"I read the card."

"Oh . . . well, I figured you would, but please just tear it up and throw it away, okay? I shouldn't have sent it."

Carla said, "This is our daughter, Julie."

"Pleased to meet you," said Julie, extending her hand.

"Pleased to meet you, too, little girl," I said enthusiastically.

"I'm not a little girl," Julie corrected me. "I'm a young lady."

"A young lady!" I said, putting both hands on my cheeks, feigning surprise. "I had no idea!" My attempt at humor thudded in the strained silence. "What I meant to say . . . *young lady* . . . is that I didn't realize you were so . . . so grown up!"

Julie stared at me. "I have a Barbie doll," she said.

"Really?"

"And I'm getting a Ken doll for my birthday."

"That's nice," I said, nodding politely.

"Are you hungry, Jos?" Carla asked.

"Are you kidding? I'm a college student. I'm always hungry."

"When will dinner be ready, hon?" asked Junior.

"Mac, please! I just put the potatoes in the oven!"

"Understood," said Junior calmly.

"I'll call you when it's ready." She and Julie disappeared into the kitchen.

I looked quizzically at my brother. "Mac?"

He shrugged. "I don't go by Junior anymore. Come on. Let's have a seat in the den. What can I get you to drink?"

"You got any ginger ale?"

"Sure thing."

We walked into the den, a cozy-looking room with wood paneling on the walls and a deep shag carpet. The bay window along one wall framed a view of a well-manicured lawn with lilac bushes and tall shade trees. "Your house is really nice, Junior . . . er, Mac."

"Have a seat." He motioned to a lime-green sofa as he headed to a bar in the corner to get my drink.

"Nice-looking chair," I said, noticing the blue upholstered recliner.

"That's my Reclina-Rocker," said Junior proudly.

"Reclina-Rocker?"

"Yeah, you can recline back in it and rock at the same time. La-Z-Boy just came out with 'em."

"What will they think of next?" I said.

"Here you go," said Junior, handing me a glass.

"Thanks," I said.

"So what're you studying in college?"

"Pre-law," I said in a decisive tone of voice.

"Interesting. You've got to study hard to be a lawyer," said Junior, demonstrating the features of his Reclina-Rocker.

"I do study hard."

"Wheaton. That's a Christian college, right?"

"Yep."

"So what does a *Christian* do in a secular profession like law?"

"Well, he tells the truth for one thing."

"That's what the witness does, Jos, not the lawyers."

"Lawyers take an oath, too, you know."

"Really?" said Junior with an odd smile. "To do what?"

"They swear to be honest and faithful in discharging their duties, for starters."

"But they always find a loophole, right?" Junior laughed at his own joke and reclined as far as he could go. I was beginning to feel that my decision to see him had not been such a good idea after all. Interacting with an older brother—not to mention one old enough to be your father—can be intimidating in the best of circumstances.

"Why do you want to be a lawyer, anyway?" Junior continued.

"I like analyzing things, getting to the heart of a matter." I paused a moment. "And I want to be rich."

Junior chuckled.

"I'm serious," I said. I looked around the room. "You've done well for yourself from the looks of it. Well, I want to do the same. Who knows? Maybe I'll do better. I have a plan in place and things seem to be working out so far."

"What's your plan?"

"Get my law degree, start practicing, join a high-profile firm, and start earning good money. Then I want to go into politics."

"Not very original," remarked Junior. "But if you can make it work, that's what counts, right?"

"I don't want to live like Mom and Dad."

"Yeah, well, I don't blame you."

I nursed my ginger ale. "Dad says you're joining the Peace Corps. That's really something."

"Yeah, isn't it?" said Junior.

"How did that happen?"

"I was over at the University of Michigan last year when John Kennedy was giving a campaign speech. He got everybody fired up about going overseas to make the world a better place. So I responded. Maybe it's like when you became a Christian. I don't know."

"Dad is a Christian now too," I said.

Silence.

"Look, Junior . . . sorry, Mac." I was trying to keep it straight. "I don't know much about what happened on the farm between you and Dad. I mean, I guess a lot of things went wrong before I was even born. You must have had your reasons . . ."

"Good reasons," Mac interrupted me.

"Good reasons," I echoed. "I just wanted you to know I've made my peace with Dad, and I didn't want to let any more time go by without trying to make peace with you."

"Peace with me?" My brother stopped rocking, although he didn't look at me. "I don't have a grievance with you, Jos."

"I guess what I mean to say, Mac, is that *I've* had a grievance with *you*. You got a lot out of Dad—more than your fair share, in my opinion. What I've resented more than anything else is that you left the family when we needed you most. But just like I told Dad, I'll tell you. Not long ago, I realized I have another Father . . . a heavenly Father who loves me and is passionate about having a relationship with me."

"I'm glad you've found something to believe in," Mac said.

"Not only that, Mac," I continued. "He's passionate about having a relationship with you, too."

"As I see it, Jos, there's not that much difference between us."

"What do you mean?"

Mac pulled the lever on the side of his chair and sat up. "Everybody looks for meaning in life," he said. "Some come to the conclusion that there is no meaning. Others find purpose in religion, like you have. Some find fulfillment in helping others, like me. There are many rivers, but they all flow into one sea, don't they?"

"I don't know about that, but I do know that Dad is a different man."

Mac's face darkened. I sensed he was about to say something when Carla's voice broke the momentary silence. "Dinner's ready!"

We enjoyed a nice meal together, with Mac filling me in on their plans with the Peace Corps.

"I read that Richard Nixon considers the Peace Corps a haven for draft dodgers," I said.

Mac laughed. "Now there's a lawyer for you to follow. And a politician. I suppose he's rich, too."

Carla set down her knife and fork. "Are you studying to be a lawyer, Jos?"

"Sure am."

"And a politician?"

"We'll just have to see what the future brings," I said with a smile.

"Well, I hope you won't be like Nixon."

"I don't see what's so bad about him, apart from his five o'clock shadow."

"I think what Jos really wants to be is a minister," said Mac.

"I never said that!" I protested.

"You don't need to say it. It's obvious, isn't it, brother?"

I couldn't think of a clever comeback. My older brother had gotten the upper hand—again. I went to bed early that night and left the next morning for Wheaton. Things hadn't worked out exactly as I had planned, but I was glad I had made the effort to reconnect with my brother. *God, keep them safe in Africa*, I prayed. *And make them a blessing.*

14

Senior Year

WHEATON COLLEGE'S PRESIDENT, Dr. Raymond Edman, a World War I veteran and former missionary to the Quichua Indians in Ecuador, knew the importance of both the spiritual and the academic health of the college. Early in his tenure he instituted Spiritual Emphasis Week as an integral part of the school calendar in the fall. During my senior year, our main speaker for that anticipated week was Wheaton alumnus Richard Halverson, pastor of Fourth Presbyterian Church in Bethesda, Maryland.

"You are among the best and brightest of the land," declared Dr. Halverson during his final address of the week. "But are you willing to obey and go? Are you willing to heed the call of God as expressed in Isaiah chapter 6?"

The entire student body was packed into the brand-new

Edman Chapel, listening closely. I was sitting in the middle of the auditorium next to Dick Purnell and Frank Kifer. Dr. Halverson's comments were making me uncomfortable. But he kept hammering away.

"I'm looking at some here today called to be engineers. You know who you are. You love calculus and physics. When you sleep at night, you dream in mathematical equations! You're gifted! But are you willing to lay it all before Him? I see doctors here today . . . and businessmen . . . I see lawyers and politicians . . . I see educators and musicians. It matters not the field of service, my friends. What matters is your willingness to bring your gifts to the altar. Who will heed the Lord's call as found in Isaiah chapter 6? Who will put his gifts on the altar and say, 'Here am I, Lord; send me'!"

I looked around at my classmates. One by one, they were getting to their feet and going down to the front, consecrating their lives and abilities to God's service. I actually saw one student pull his slide rule from his pocket and lay it at Dr. Halverson's feet. Dick, who was a pre-med student, stood up and pushed past me, followed by Frank. More and more students were making their way down the aisles.

I got up too—and half ran out of the building.

My roommates found me later in my bed, with the covers pulled over my head. "What do you want?" I demanded.

"Are you all right?" Dick asked. I didn't answer.

"Josh, are you all right?" he repeated.

"Leave me alone," I said. He heeded my words and

I heard his footsteps receding. Later that night, I got up and walked around the campus. It was close to midnight when I sat down in the twenty-four-hour diner Round the Clock on the corner of Wesley and Hale streets in downtown Wheaton. *I'm tired,* I said to myself. And coffee wasn't going to help. It wasn't physical tiredness. I was tired of pretending.

I couldn't get Dr. Halverson's words out of my head. "Who will heed the Lord's call as found in Isaiah chapter 6? Who will put his gifts on the altar and say, 'Here am I, Lord; send me'!"

As a Christian, all I had ever heard was that God wanted to use my talents and abilities for His glory. But what did I have to offer God? A string of failures! I was aware of the contradiction. Many people thought I had a bright future ahead. I was getting good grades, and several of my teachers thought I'd make an excellent lawyer. Maybe so. But was I an excellent Christian? There were just too many broken pieces in my life, and it seemed I would never be able to overcome my feeling of deep inferiority, which often manifested itself in my stuttering or poor grammar. I still carried the scars of sexual abuse and physical violence and family brokenness that colored every aspect of my life and affected all my relationships. And while I might succeed in hiding those flaws and limitations from others, how could I hide them from myself? I still had to look at the man in the mirror.

Yes, Pastor Logan, you're right. The Christian life is a marathon and it is meant to be run with perseverance.

And I cannot run anymore.

I left the diner and just started walking. It was mid-autumn, and a refreshing coolness hung in the air. On and on I walked, not thinking about where I was going. The dry leaves crunched under my feet as jarring memories, sins, and temptations that I thought had long been buried in baptism with Christ rose up to assault me with near-physical intensity. I felt condemned, and it seemed more than I could bear. I only hoped my dad wouldn't hear that I had walked away from the Lord.

I imagined Pastor Logan beside me. He would know what to do. He would know how to counsel me. But he wasn't here. All I could see in my mind were his kind, searching eyes, which seemed to be filled with infinite pity.

It was probably around four in the morning when I stopped under a street lamp on Union Street. I was remembering the story in the Bible of the child who had a few fish and loaves of bread and offered them to feed the hungry multitude. I felt like that boy. But there was a difference. There was no miracle in my life to turn the little I had into something more.

"God," I said without thinking about it, "deep in my heart, I want to serve You, but what can I bring You? Let's be honest. I have nothing worthwhile to offer You. I have no great gifts or abilities in anything, and I'm deeply wounded by the past. But if You're willing, let this place be an altar tonight, and let me lay down here what I am not. I give You what I lack, Lord. I give You what I don't have. You can't take my strengths because I don't have any to give You. You can't take my abilities because they're not really there. But if You're willing, Lord . . . if You're willing to take my weaknesses and failings, and glorify Yourself through them, O God, I promise I'll serve You the rest of my life with every breath I take."

I don't know how long I stood there or what else I might have prayed, but I remember walking across the Wheaton campus as the eastern sky was showing a hint of light, signaling the dawn. The terrible burden of sin and condemnation had lifted from me, and I was prepared to greet the day. I was back in the race.

Less than three weeks later, I met someone who coached me for the spiritual marathon ahead.

• • •

Bill Bright was clearly a man on a mission, energized by the great commission to evangelize the world before the second coming of Jesus Christ. He had spoken at Wheaton's chapel service while on a recruiting trip for the organization he had founded ten years earlier: Campus Crusade for Christ. Now a half dozen of us were seated around him at a table in the student cafeteria, wanting to know more about him and his organization.

"I'd like to share a concept with you that has the potential to transform not only your lives, but those of everyone you meet," he told us. We clustered in closer together as he picked up a napkin and reached for a pen inside his coat pocket. "There are basically three kinds of people in the world. I'm referring to women as well as men, but for the purpose of this illustration, we'll refer to these three kinds of people as the natural man, the carnal man, and the spiritual man."

He drew three circles side by side on the napkin and what looked like a chair in the middle of each of the circles. "Here you have the natural man," he said, pointing to the first of the circles and drawing an *s* on the seat of the chair. "The natural man has put self on the throne." Mr. Bright penned a *t* close to the circle, but on the outside of it. As he continued speaking, I realized it was not a *t* but a cross, representing Jesus.

"Jesus is outside this man's world," he said, pointing to the cross. "Perhaps the man's never been introduced to the Lord; perhaps he's rejected Him as Savior. But Christ is not in this man's life."

Mr. Bright's finger was on the second circle. "Here you have the carnal man." Again, he drew an *s* on the seat of the chair, but put the cross inside the circle at the foot of the chair.

"Like the natural man, the carnal man has also set himself on the throne. He is a Christian, but he's unfruitful. He's trusting in his own efforts to live the Christian life. With Christ off to the side, he lives a compromised life."

Mr. Bright took a sip of coffee and drew a cross on the chair in the third circle. "Unlike the other two, the spiritual man puts Christ on the throne of his life and sets himself, his own ego . . ." Mr. Bright took his pen again and made an *s* at the foot of the chair, "off to the side. He embraces the fullness of the Holy Spirit and lives a victorious life in Christ. But here's a question. If I asked you how to appropriate the power of the Holy Spirit, would you know what to do?"

"I guess the first thing I'd do is make sure that Christ is sitting on the throne of my life," said Frank.

"Excellent," said Mr. Bright. "For those of you who play basketball, that's called getting into position." He looked around the table. "Who can name the fruits of the Holy Spirit for me?"

Dick Purnell rattled them off rapidly before any of the rest of us could get a word in: "Love, joy, peace, patience, kindness, goodness, faithfulness, gentleness, self-control."

Show-off, I thought.

Mr. Bright nodded enthusiastically, saying, "These are precisely the qualities that come to the fore when we place Christ on the throne of our life and ask the Holy Spirit to fill us and keep filling us."

"Keep filling us?" I asked.

"The Holy Spirit wants to fill you to overflowing, son. You and the Holy Spirit have a job to do!" Mr. Bright looked around at the group. We waited for him to continue.

"Boys, I'm from Oklahoma originally, and in that part of the country, we do a lot of drilling for oil. Well, there was once an old Texas cowboy who didn't ride the range anymore and lived in the most abject poverty on a piece of land off in the middle of nowhere. When he died, an exploration company discovered oil on his property. It was a huge reserve, and it would have made the old cowboy a millionaire many times over. The oil was buried on his land, and he'd been sitting on top of it the whole time but didn't know it. And he died penniless. The power of the Holy Spirit is like that oil. If you belong to Christ, the Spirit already lives inside you, poised to rise up in you like a . . . like a gusher of oil, I suppose! But you need to tap into His power. And you do that through prayer."

Mr. Bright looked directly at me. "Would you like to receive the power of the Holy Spirit?"

"Now?" I asked.

"Right now."

"Yes, sir, I would."

Mr. Bright went around the table, asking each of us the same question. Everyone said yes and we bowed our heads as Mr. Bright prayed, "Dear Father, we need You. We acknowledge that we've been directing our own lives and, as a result, have sinned against You. We humbly thank You that through Christ we have forgiveness of sins. Now, through faith, we invite Jesus Christ to take His rightful place on the throne of our individual lives. We ask You now—again by faith—to fill us to overflowing with the Holy Spirit as You have promised to do in Your Word. We thank and praise You. In Christ's name, amen."

"Amen," everyone said.

"Now breathe in," said Mr. Bright, taking a deep breath.

Everyone breathed in. "Now breathe out." We exhaled together. He repeated the exercise. "Breathe in the Holy Spirit," he said, "and exhale your sin. Get rid of it. Again, breathe in God's forgiveness. Receive the gracious Holy Spirit." He paused and looked around at us. "The Holy Spirit is a person; remember that. He has come to comfort us, counsel us, and empower us to be His witnesses to the ends of the earth. And now, gentlemen, I need to catch a train to New York. It's been an absolute pleasure meeting you, and I'm sure I'll be seeing some of you again."

"Thank you for praying with us," I said, standing to my feet and shaking his hand.

"My pleasure, . . ." he paused, expecting me to say my name.

"Josh. Josh McDowell."

Mr. Bright nodded. "Remember to breathe, Josh."

"Oh, I'll remember!"

"Just as you breathe physically, you need to breathe spiritually. It's not something you do once and then forget about doing again. It's ongoing—day in and day out. It's something to follow the rest of your life."

"I understand, sir. Like a marathon."

Mr. Bright gave me a curious look, grabbed his briefcase, and left for the train station.

15

Engagement and Graduation

I TOOK ONLY ENOUGH CHANGE to the pay phone to talk for five minutes. I wasn't trying to be a cheapskate. I just didn't have the courage to talk to Mr. Merrick any longer than that. Mrs. Merrick answered and put her husband on the phone.

"Hello?"

"Mr. Merrick?"

"Yes."

"Hello, sir. This is Josh McDowell."

"Well, hello, Josh. Good to hear from you. How're things at Wheaton?"

"Good, sir. Very good."

"I'm pleased to hear that. Grades holding up?"

"Uh, yes, sir. The grades are . . . I'm getting good grades, sir."

"Excellent. And how are plans shaping up for law school?"

"Good, sir! Very good. I, uh . . . I'm looking at different law schools now."

"Well, that's terrific, Josh. I suppose you want to talk with Lynne?"

"Uh, yes, sir, I do, but, uh, I'd, uh . . . I'd like to talk to you, too."

"Of course."

"Mr. Merrick, . . . I'd like to marry your daughter."

The silence on the other end of the line was excruciating. I nervously rubbed my remaining quarters together, which were getting hot and slippery from my sweaty palms.

"Well, Josh," Mr. Merrick said at last, "I know my daughter loves you. I've tried to help her understand that marriage is much, much more than fuzzy feelings and stars in the eyes."

"Yes, sir."

"Not only that, when I first met you, I did not approve of you seeing Lynne."

"Yes, sir, I know."

"But I tell you what. You have certainly changed in my estimation over this last year and a half, and I would be very pleased to give my permission for you to marry my daughter."

"Thank you, sir."

"Now do you want to talk with the young lady?"

"I do, sir. Yes, I do. Thank you very much, sir."

"You're welcome." Mr. Merrick set down the phone, and by the time Lynne picked it up, I was nearly out of change.

"Hello?" she said.

"Lynne, will you marry me?"

"Of course I will!" she said.

And with that, the phone died.

Two weeks later, Lynne drove to Wheaton with her sister, Angie, and spent the night at a guesthouse in town. The next day was Saturday, the first weekend in May, and I was as nervous as a cat. There was a long-standing tradition at Wheaton College for couples to celebrate their engagement or marriage by "going up the tower" at Blanchard Hall and ringing the bell to let everyone on campus know. Earlier in the week I had gotten permission from the student activities office to reserve the tower for the festivities, and I spent Saturday morning making the necessary preparations with Dick, Frank, and some of my other friends. We had a cake to pick up, some bottles of sparkling grape juice, cups, plates, forks, and napkins.

We were ready a few minutes before ten o'clock, but there was no sign of Lynne. We waited. And we waited. The clock struck eleven.

"What time did you tell her to be here?" asked Frank.

"Ten o'clock," I said.

"Lesson number one," said Dick ominously. "Women are never on time."

"Be to her virtues very kind, to her faults a little blind," said Frank.

"Did you just make that up?" I asked.

"Of course not," scoffed Dick. "That's a line from that French poet . . . what's his name?"

"Matthew Prior, you numbskull! He wasn't French; he was English."

"Quiet! Both of you!" I warned. We could hear someone coming up the steps of the tower. And then, a few moments later, appeared the girl I was going to marry. Behind Lynne was her sister, Angie, and a female friend who was a sophomore at Wheaton.

"Let's get this show on the road," said Dick, popping open the grape juice and pouring a glass. "I have a toast to make." He waited impatiently while everyone was served and then made his toast. "To Josh and Lynne. May you experience many years of wedded bliss. And don't forget this one secret for a happy marriage . . ."

"As if he knows," cracked Frank under his breath.

"No man is truly and happily married until he understands every word his wife is *not* saying!"

"What does that mean?" asked Frank, clearing his throat and proposing his own toast. "Josh. Lynne. We're happy for you on this auspicious day. Just remember that you're not getting married because you'll be able to live with each other. You're getting married because there's no way you can live without each other."

"Hear, hear," said my friend Jim Green, raising his glass while the ladies made soft, cooing sounds of approbation. I took Lynne's hands in mine and we looked deep into each other's eyes. And I knew . . . beyond any doubt . . . I was making the wrong decision.

Some people talk about how their life flashes before them when they're about to die. I had experienced that myself when my car was rear-ended by the drunk driver. Now I was undergoing a similar experience, but this time it was my future that flashed in front of me. Lynne was a marvelous and beautiful girl, but I didn't love her the way I should. *The way I should? What does that mean?* I didn't know what it meant. I only knew there was a real and undeniable feeling deep inside me that I was about to do something I'd regret for the rest of my life. I was half-tempted to call it off right there, but I was in too deep, and I knew that I couldn't end things now without breaking someone's heart. I took out the ring I had bought for Lynne in Battle Creek and slipped it on her finger.

Lynne began to cry. She didn't have a clue as to what I was thinking, and neither did anyone else.

"Pull the rope, Josh," Dick urged me. I nodded, looking at the rope hanging from the tower bell, which suddenly resembled a hangman's noose. Once at a wedding, I saw one of the groomsmen faint dead away. Right there in front of everybody. I couldn't let that happen to me. I'd never live it down. With a forced smile, I took hold of the rope and steadied myself. And then I pulled the rope down hard—seven times.

Lynne did the same, ringing the bell seven times. In between the rings, true to Wheaton college tradition, we could hear the shouts of several guys who happened to be walking past Blanchard Hall. Their catcalls were predictable.

"Don't do it!" I heard one voice off in the distance.

"Good-bye, freedom!" cried another, closer at hand. "Welcome, ball and chain!"

Laughing it all off, Lynne and I both took hold of the rope and pulled together another seven times. Seven. The number of perfection.

"Here, guys." Angie handed us a marker to add our names to the hundreds of others scrawled on the bell tower wall. *Josh and Lynne. Engaged May 5, Married*

"What date do we write for the marriage, honey?" asked Lynne, smiling at me sweetly, the marker ready.

Never, I wanted to scream. *You're a great gal, Lynne, the sweetest girl I've ever known. But this will never work. You're a homebody and I want to travel the world!*

"How about Leap Year?" I said jokingly.

Lynne wrote *Very Soon* and we kissed each other. I was rolling down a hill like a snowball.

• • •

There was one thing I could be thankful for—Lynne went back home to Michigan while I finished out my senior year. She wrote me numerous letters, none of which I answered, and we talked several times on the phone. She had to know something was wrong. I was evasive about most everything; I just didn't have the courage to tell her about my deep misgivings.

The closest I got to it was to tell her during the course of one of those phone calls that I wasn't sure if I really loved her. Her response was completely disarming. "I understand, darling. Don't worry. Feelings can be so misleading. It'll all come together in time, you'll see."

Mercifully, I was too distracted with my studies and final exams and part-time work to worry much about what would happen between us. Perhaps she was right. Perhaps it would all come together in time. One thing was certain. I did not understand love. Or women. Maybe both.

Our commencement speaker was none other than Billy Graham. He had graduated from Wheaton nineteen years earlier and was conducting a crusade at the sprawling McCormick Place convention center in Chicago. He broke away to address us on Monday morning, June 11.

"There is a world out there still waiting for the man who is wholly yielded to God," he said toward the end of his remarks. "There's a world out there where hospitals need to be built, where students need to be taught, where sermons need to be preached, where Elijahs and John the Baptists are needed. Yes, there are frontiers to conquer. And God will be with us."

Tall and handsome, his wide-set eyes flashing with the passion of his beliefs, he seemed to me like an angel speaking in a Southern accent. Unlike the previous autumn, I didn't get up and run out of the auditorium in dismay. I looked around at my peers, feeling pride in all our accomplishments, realizing that we formed one body working together to take the gospel to the ends of the earth. In one regard, however, I was conspicuous. My neck had been giving me problems for days, and I had to wear the bulky white brace to the ceremony.

16

A Final Summer

I DIDN'T STAY on the farm that summer. I rented a small room in Battle Creek to be near my painting business. It was a good decision overall because work was going really well and I needed to stay close to the business side of things. But there were other reasons for avoiding my familiar haunts.

The truth is, I didn't want to stay at home because of the memories it conjured up, especially those of the mother who was no longer there. I continued to agonize over where, in fact, she was—or might be. *There is an afterlife,* I said to myself. *There is a heaven and a hell. And if someone rejects Christ in this lifetime, that person is not going to heaven.* My teachers had taught me well.

My thoughts turned again to Mom. I'm sure she would

have attended church more often if my father hadn't been a drunkard. Mom had treated the Bible with respect, calling it a "holy book." *Doesn't that count for something, God?* Sadly, I knew the answer all too well: we are not saved by good deeds or good intentions. Salvation is through faith and trust in Christ alone.

So where did that put Mom? She was gone, and the man who had done more than anyone else to keep her from the embrace of Christ was enjoying not only a new spiritual life but a new wife as well. It didn't seem fair. It was as if my mother had sacrificed herself for someone else to come to Christ and then had been tossed to the side. *Why is it that the people who deserve to suffer least are the ones who seem to suffer most in this world?*

I also wanted to keep a low profile in and around Athens and Factoryville because of Lynne. What a terrible thing to admit! If there had been a shadow of doubt before, I was now convinced I would never be able to marry her, although I was still trying to figure out how I was going to break the news to her. Secretly, I was hoping the problem would just take care of itself, without a confrontation. I knew that was unrealistic on my part, as well as unfair to Lynne.

But I couldn't find the courage to tell her face-to-face, so I took refuge in my long hours at work, as well as making all the necessary plans to attend UCLA law school in the fall. Bob Hammond, an old friend from Kellogg Community College, was the impetus behind the realization of that dream. He had become a Christian and worked for me at the painting company. As we talked one day, I discovered he planned to go to California at the end of the summer.

"We should head out together," said Bob.

"When are you leaving?" I asked.

"I'll leave tomorrow if you want to."

"I'll need more time than that, hipster. I'm runnin' a business here."

"How much time d'you need?"

"Three weeks?"

"Three weeks it is. We can drive my Cadillac and tow your MG."

"Really?"

"Sure. Why not? We'll split the travel expenses fifty-fifty. How does that sound? I have some friends in California. They'll let us crash at their place until we find something."

"Sounds promising," I said.

"So are you in?"

"I'm in."

Bob gave me a punch on the arm. "Heading west, young man!" he said to me exuberantly. "Heading west!"

"Yeah, yeah, I got it. Now you head west and finish painting that wall. You still work for the Superior Painting Company, and you've got a house to finish up."

Bob gave me a mock salute and went back to work. The weeks passed, and I finally worked up the nerve to visit Lynne after work one day. I knocked on the door and she answered it.

"Hi, Lynne."

"Hi, Josh. Come in."

"Can we talk out here? I mean, it's such a nice evening and all."

"Sure." Lynne sat in the love seat swing, leaving room for me to join her. I leaned against the railing on the veranda instead. "Lynne, I've come by to tell you that . . . uh . . . next week . . ."

"Yes?"

"Next week . . ." I felt a stutter coming on.

"What about next week?"

"I'm . . . uh . . . leave . . . leaving for . . . for . . . California." I finally got it out.

"Isn't that early to leave for law school?"

I took a deep breath and tried to collect myself. "It's quite a distance, you know, and . . . and Bob . . . Bob Hammond and I are planning to do some . . . some sightseeing along the way. The Rockies, the Grand Canyon, all that."

"Bob Hammond?"

"He works for me at the painting company."

"Send me a postcard, okay?"

"Lynne . . ."

She looked at me. I could see her eyes glistening in the dark.

"Lynne. I'm sorry . . ."

Lynne put her finger on my lips to stop me from speaking further, but the words came out anyway. "I can't marry you, Lynne. I just can't."

Finally, we could tell each other what was really on our minds.

"You loved me once, didn't you?"

"Yes, I did."

"Then what's changed? I still love you."

"Lynne," I said, sitting down beside her, "you and I are believers. We believe that Jesus will guide our steps. We pray for His will to be done in our lives . . ."

"There must be a reason," she said firmly, interrupting me.

"I know how your parents are."

"My parents should have nothing to do with this."

"But they will. They're not going to want you to live far away from home, whereas I want to get as far away from here as possible. Who knows where we might end up? It could be halfway around the world. Not only that, law school is going to demand everything from me for the next several years."

"Then I'll wait."

"I don't want to get married, Lynne. If it helps at all, there's no one else in my life."

Lynne looked straight ahead. "Anything else?"

"Only that I am deeply sorry for the pain I have caused you. I never meant to do that."

"I think you should go now, Josh."

"Lynne, ah, about the ring . . ."

"What about it?"

"Well, now that we're not getting married, do you think I could have it back?"

• • •

Lynne kept the ring.

And rather than risk running into her again around town or at church, I called Bob and asked him if we could leave a few days earlier than planned. We agreed on a Friday morning departure, and I drove over to my dad's house the afternoon before. Berta was in the kitchen preparing dinner.

"He's fishing over at Union Lake," she informed me.

Sure enough, I found Dad by the lake with his little cooler and fishing pole. "Hi, Dad. Catch anything?" I called to him.

"A few. But nothing like when you and I were here. You come to fish? I only have the one pole."

"Nah, Dad, that's fine. I didn't come to go fishing."

"Oh."

"I'm leaving for California tomorrow."

"Oh, I thought you wasn't goin' til end of next week."

"Plans changed."

"That has a way of happenin', don't it," said Dad. "When're you comin' back?"

"It doesn't make much sense to come home for Thanksgiving. Maybe Christmas?"

Dad looked at me awhile without saying anything. Gradually, a smile formed on his lips. "Let me know if I can do anything."

"Like what?"

"If you get into financial troubles out there—"

"You don't have any money, Dad."

"I have a little bit tucked away. And if we need to, I can sell off some more of the farm."

I shook my head. "The farm is your home. I'll be fine. Just take care of yourself, okay?"

"If you ever need some free advice . . ."

"I'll ask you, right?"

"You betcha. But add a lotta salt to whatever I say."

I nodded. Suddenly, the pole nearly jumped out of Dad's hand. He hadn't been paying attention when the fish grabbed the hook. A few seconds later, he had a nice-size bluegill added to his cooler. He rebaited the hook, cast again, and—bam!—another fish. "Gee willikers, Jos! You stand right over here, son! You're bringin' me good luck!"

I stayed with Dad until dark, then walked back with him to the farmhouse in the moonlight. Berta insisted I eat some dinner, even though it had grown cold. I didn't object. As I wolfed down the food, Dad excused himself and reappeared with an old toolbox.

"Do you need help with something, Dad?" I asked.

"Nah, I'm good. But I want you to take this with you to California. It might come in handy along the way."

I was about to tell Dad that both Bob and I already had our own tool kits, but thought better of it. He set the box on the table next to me.

"Wilmot!" protested Berta. "Not on the dining room table! That's a clean tablecloth."

I picked up the toolbox and set it on the floor next to my feet.

"Men." Berta brushed away some telltale rust and dirt that had been left behind.

"Thanks, Dad," I said. "I'll bring it back when I come home."

"No, son. I don't want you to bring it back. It belongs to you now."

"From father to son," I said.

"From father to son," repeated Dad.

We visited a little longer, but then it was time to go. "Take good care of him, Berta," I said at the door.

"Oh, I will, Jos, you know that." Berta kissed me on the cheek and I walked out of the house I had grown up in—been born in, as a matter of fact. I took a last look at the weathered walls, the screen door that had slammed behind me who knows how many times, and the porch and steps that could use a coat of paint. I thought of that verse in the Bible: *When I was a child, I spoke as a child, I understood as a child, I thought as a child; but when I became a man, I put away childish things*. As I walked to my car, I marveled at how peaceful looking everything seemed in the moonlight. In a quiet part of my heart, I whispered, *Good-bye*.

Dad handed me the toolbox. He had insisted on carrying it himself. I'm not sure if he thought I was going to forget it or intentionally leave it behind.

"Keep sharing your testimony with folks around town," I said as we walked along. "In the prisons, too."

"I'll do that, son."

"You're having an impact on a lot of people's lives."

Dad nodded, his lips drawn.

"Are you all right, Dad? You don't look so good."

"I'm fine," he said. "Just my stomach sometimes. All the drinking over the years, I guess."

"You need to have a doctor check that out," I said, putting the toolbox in the backseat. As I got into the car, Dad put his hands on the driver's side door, leaning down to see me better. "When you come at Christmas, we'll go ice fishin' up at Manistique."

"Sure thing."

"We'll plan ahead of time so you won't have no excuses."

"There won't be any excuses, Dad."

He nodded.

Now we see dimly in a mirror, but one day we'll see face-to-face. Now, I know in part; but then I'll know fully even as I am also known.

"Well, I guess this is good-bye for now," said Dad. "Send me your address when you get settled. I'll write you."

Wow, I thought. *A letter from my dad. That'll be a first.* "You bet," I said. I started the car and backed up. Dad was visible briefly in the side-view mirror, illuminated by the taillights. He looked pale and ghostly, waving a final time before fading from view in the darkness.

And now remain these three—faith, hope, love. But the greatest of these is love.

17

Out West

BOB AND I LEFT Battle Creek midmorning the next day. It was sunny and clear, and we took our time on the long drive through Indiana and Illinois. A few days later, we reached Iowa, then Nebraska and Colorado. Eight or nine days had passed by the time we skirted the Utah border and crossed into Arizona, our sights set on the Grand Canyon.

We ended up on the south rim and decided to hike with a guided tour group. The views were spectacular along the way. So were the sheer drops over the edge! We shared the trail with mules carrying the less-intrepid tourists, so there were times when we were hugging the sides of the cliff to make room. It was a breathtaking marvel of nature, overwhelming evidence that God has revealed His invisible qualities through the things He has made.

Before we knew it, we found ourselves mixed in with a group of foreign exchange students. I was drawn to them immediately and began making small talk. There was Pascoal from Mozambique, Marwan from Egypt, Ingvar from Sweden, and Gina from Italy, among others.

When we stopped for lunch at Indian Garden, about four and a half miles down the trail, I was struck with an overwhelming urge to share more about my faith with the others. It was a beautiful setting. Indian Garden, once home to the Havasupai Indian tribe, is an oasis amidst the towering walls of the canyon. Garden Creek winds its way through the respite, shaded by massive cottonwood trees. As everyone got comfortable, I continued the conversation about our different religious beliefs that had started when we were hiking together.

"Can I tell you about the God of the Bible?" I asked. When no one objected, I directed their attention to our surroundings. "All around us we can see the beauty of God's creation. We can see that He is a God of power, a God of beauty and design. But have you ever stopped to think that we, too, are the work of His hands, just like these gorgeous cliffs we see? The Bible says He made us all—Pascoal from Mozambique, Marwan from Egypt, Ingvar from Sweden . . . Gina, I think you might be from heaven, but still . . ." Everyone laughed.

"And me? Well, I'm just a farm boy from Michigan of humble Irish and English stock. But we're each beautiful to God. He made each one of us in His image, you see. He enjoys our company, and we should enjoy His! He's a loving and holy Father. But our sins have separated us from Him. There's a gulf that exists between us and God. So how do we reach Him? How do we make peace with Him? The answer is in Jesus, the Savior, who died on a cross that we might go free."

I glanced at Bob. His mouth had dropped open in astonishment, partly because of my boldness but also because everyone seemed to be hanging on every word I said. I probably talked another five minutes and then sat down. Bob passed me a sandwich, but I was too excited to eat. Several students started asking me questions, and I was thrilled to continue the dialogue. Before long, it was time for us to hike back up to the summit.

"How long have you been a public speaker?" asked Ingvar, falling in beside me.

"He's a preacher, not a public speaker," said Wallace, a student from New Zealand.

"Actually, I'm neither one. I'm just a student like you guys."

"Are you studying theology?" asked Pascoal.

"No. I'm going to law school in California."

"I have an uncle in Sweden who is a Lutheran minister," said Ingvar. "He and his wife talk about Jesus the way you do."

"That's because they must know Him, Ingvar. No doubt He's living in their hearts by faith and they're in love with

Him. When you get to know Jesus as Savior and Lord, you always fall in love with Him."

"I am not a believer, you understand," said Ingvar. "I guess I would call myself an agnostic."

"I was a member of that club too!" I said cheerily, going on to tell them about the challenge I had been given and how I had discovered the truth of Jesus' existence during my journey across Europe.

By the time we arrived at the top, we were all exhausted. But we had conquered part of the Grand Canyon together and were laughing and joking around, despite how taxing it had been. I had blisters on both feet and a sunburn, but most important, invitations to visit newfound friends in seven different countries.

"You sure do have the gift of gab when it gets hold of you," Bob said to me when we were back on the road.

I smiled, but for the moment I reveled in the serenity of the landscape across the open range, with a striking sunset in front of us and the wind blowing through my hair. The future lay ahead, a world of promise.

It doesn't get much better than this, I thought. *Thank You, God, for calling me as Your own and pulling me out of my bitterness and unbelief. There was a time when I was no different from any of the students we just met at the Grand Canyon. Let me never forget that. What a joy to talk with them! I hope something I said today has stuck with them. I belong to You, Lord. Here I come to do Your will.*

Even if it's ministry?

The random question in my mind almost sounded audible. I sat up, momentarily startled.

Bob looked over at me. "You all right?"

"Yeah, I'm fine."

"You sure? You look funny."

"No, I'm fine. Just thinking about things."

We reached Costa Mesa two days later and stayed with a Christian friend of Bob's, who made both of us feel at home.

The evening after we arrived, I picked up a magazine in the house, and when I thumbed through it, I noticed a small advertisement for Talbot Theological Seminary in La Mirada, California. As I looked at the ad, I had what some might call a premonition. *Does God want me to go here? Wait a minute. Why am I even thinking such a thing? I'm set on law school, and law school it's going to be.*

This "incident" happened around eight o'clock at night. When I woke up the next morning, the magazine ad was still nagging me. *I guess it wouldn't hurt to drive over to La Mirada and give the place a quick look.* It was a forty-minute drive, and on the way there, I made a pact with God: *If for some crazy reason they accept me today, I'll know it's Your will for me to go into ministry. Otherwise, I'm entering law school as planned.*

There. That was simple.

It was a sunny day, and I drove down the Santa Ana Freeway feeling good about life. I reached La Mirada and pulled into the seminary's parking lot next to the administration building. When I found the registrar's office, I told the receptionist I was interested in going to seminary.

"Your name?" she asked.

"McDowell. Josh McDowell."

She looked through her files and shook her head. "I'm sorry. We don't have an application for you."

"Oh, I know, I know. Fact is, I never heard about your school until last night."

The receptionist's eyes widened. "And you were thinking you'd . . . do what?"

"Sign up and start school. But I guess I can't do that, can I?"

"Certainly not. The application process takes several months, and even that's fast. You wouldn't be able to start classes until next year. At the earliest."

I breathed a sigh of relief. "Perfect."

"What's that?"

"Have a nice day, ma'am," I said, turning to leave. *There,* I said to myself as I walked toward the door. *I've kept my part of the bargain. UCLA, here I come.*

But for some reason I stopped, then walked back to the receptionist's desk. She was still looking at me, probably wondering if she should call the police. "Just to be sure, who is the last person I could talk to about this?"

"That would be Dr. Feinberg."

"Feinberg?"

"But you can't talk to him."

"Why not?"

"He's the dean."

"Is he here?"

"He's not normally here in the summer, but . . ."

"Yes?"

"He is here today. He came in unexpectedly."

"Then why can't I talk to him?"

"I just told you. He's the dean of the seminary and an extremely busy man."

"But you could ask him for me, couldn't you?"

The receptionist glowered at me. I was getting nowhere. She gave me a defiant look, then said, "Wait here, please."

"Will do," I replied, taking a seat as she disappeared down the hall.

She returned a few minutes later. I stood up and was about to thank her for trying when I heard, "He can see you now. Last office on the left." I trudged in the direction she had come from with a sense of dread until I was finally in front of Dr. Charles Feinberg's door. It was open, and he was bent over his large desk, writing. I tapped on the door and coughed lightly.

"Come in," he said, looking up. He was middle-aged, wearing a suit and tie. His neatly trimmed mustache and thick, black-framed glasses made him look distinguished.

I walked up to him and blurted out, "I don't want to go to seminary. I want to go to law school. It's what I've dreamed about doing my entire life and I've come out here to go to UCLA but I saw this ad about your school last night in a magazine and it seems that God might be tryin' to tell me something."

"He's funny that way, isn't He?" said Dr. Feinberg, glancing out the window. "Is that your MG out there?"

I grinned. "Sure is," I said flippantly. "Shove it and love it."

"Is that so?"

"Oh, you'd better believe it. You can agitate the gravel with that baby, let me tell you."

Dr. Feinberg swiveled around in his chair and looked at me over his eyeglasses. *Good,* I thought. *I've made a bad impression.*

"So where did you do your undergraduate work, Mr. . . ."

"McDowell."

"Mr. McDowell."

"I went to Wheaton, sir."

"And your grades? How were they?"

"They were good enough."

Dr. Feinberg held his hands in front of him, tapping the tips of his fingers together. "And you're here at Talbot Seminary because you want to go to law school at UCLA."

"No, sir. I mean, yes, sir. Look, I made a bargain, okay?"

"This is getting more and more interesting," said the dean wryly.

"I told God if He wants me to go into ministry, I'll do it! I just can't believe it's what He wants." I crossed my arms and waited for Dr. Feinberg to refute what I had just said. There was a long and awkward silence. He looked at my car again, then at me.

"Call Wheaton today and have them airmail your transcripts here," he said. "You can start class on Monday, and we'll sort out the admission details over the next several weeks." Again a silence. "Will that be all right with you, Mr. McDowell?"

I didn't speak; I didn't nod my head; I don't think I even blinked. I walked out of Dr. Feinberg's office totally devastated. I had crudely engineered the entire morning, thinking I was being honest with God *and* getting my own way in the bargain. God sure had put me in my place, and I wasn't happy about it.

I started classes that Monday and attended faithfully for two weeks. But I was miserable the entire time. I tried to compensate by attending every social function I could find on campus, showing up with a different date each time. But nothing brought me lasting peace. Truth be told, I felt God had tricked me into falling headlong into a trap of my own making. But I had given Him my word and stuck with it.

As I started the third week of school, I was daydreaming in my church history class when the professor, Dr. James Christian, called me out in front of everybody. I had missed the context of his remark, but what I did hear made me livid.

"Take Mr. McDowell there, for example," Dr. Christian said, pointing in my direction. "If the church made global evangelization as much a priority as he does dating all the coeds, the entire world would be saved in our lifetime."

There were titters of laughter around me. I grabbed my books and notebook, walked up to the front of the classroom, and slammed them on the professor's desk. "I've had it!" I yelled. "I don't need to take this. I'm finished!" I stormed out of the building.

I didn't know where to go, but I knew I needed to get off campus. I walked down Biola Avenue a short distance, then came to McNally Junior High. Just as I passed by, the school bell rang and hundreds of students poured out the door. I looked at my watch. It was a few minutes before noon. I leaned against a telephone pole as the young teens dispersed in every direction in front of me. I suppose the entire school was emptied in less than a minute, but for me, the flow of human traffic seemed endless. I felt rooted to the ground and couldn't move. It was as if I were paralyzed. I could see the face of each young person so clearly, but it seemed I was invisible to them.

And then I heard a voice. I can't say whether it was actually audible or just a strong impression. Either way, it was undeniably clear. God's voice pierced my heart: *I've called you to reach young people. Do not turn away.* Plain and simple. Nothing more, nothing less. I knew that arguing would be futile.

Suddenly I remembered what Bill Bright had said about the "spiritual man." *Where is Christ in my life?* I thought. *Is He in control of my will? Is He on the throne of my life where He belongs?*

Eventually, the junior high students filed back into the building as quickly as they had come out. My temporary paralysis subsided and I returned to Talbot. I walked back into my church history class and apologized to Dr. Christian in front of everyone, then picked up my books and returned to my seat. It was 12:30. From that moment on, as I am fond of saying, "A cemetery became a seminary."

18

The Call

"YOU WANTED TO SEE ME?" I asked the receptionist in Talbot's administrative office.

"I have an urgent message for you to call home," she said. "Oh, and there's a letter for you too." I recognized the large handwriting on the envelope immediately.

"Well, what do you know," I said. "My dad wrote me a letter!"

I went to a nearby pay phone and called home. I had no idea what could be urgent enough to pull me out of class. Berta answered. "Jos . . ." her voice cracked.

"Berta? Are you all right?"

"Your dad . . ."

"What's wrong?"

"He's dead!"

"What?"

"He died yesterday."

"Died?" I repeated. I was dumbstruck. "Wha–what happened?" I finally got the words out.

"He just fell over in the barn."

Fell over in the barn. Just like my beloved horse, Dolly, had years before. I had found her one morning, legs straight up in the air, frozen in place.

"The doctor says his liver was shot," Berta continued. "All the drinkin' he had done, I guess. He just went real fast." Berta gave me the details about the memorial service. "It's going to be Thursday at Jenkins Funeral Home, and everyone in the family has asked if you would speak."

"Why me?" I asked, feeling numb.

"Because you're the religious one in the family, I s'pose," she said, still crying.

So that's how they see me. I looked at Dad's unopened letter in my hand and slowly hung up the phone. I drove to a nearby travel agency and bought a plane ticket for Detroit, leaving early in the morning. Then I went to my room and sat by the open window until it grew dark. It was Tuesday, November 13.

I quickly packed a few belongings and lay down on my bed, staring at the ceiling. Outside, I heard the plaintive hoot of an owl. Someone once said it never rains in Southern California. Obviously, that person had never visited in the fall or wintertime. I could feel the temperature dropping and smell rain in the air, the first rain in many months. It suddenly reminded me of home, and I began to cry.

On the plane the next morning, I read Dad's letter.

Dear Jos,

Thanks for sending me your address. I hope things work out for you at the seminery. As we know, God works in mighty mysterious ways to get His will done, so I wouldn't question things too much. Just do the best you can with what you got. As Jesus saith, "The night cometh, when no man can work." That's in the ninth chapter of the Gospel according to St. John, by the way.

Things are quiet here on the farm. I'm goin' to sell the rest of the pigs in a few weeks and maybe the Guernsey, too.

I been back to Jackson Penitentiary to speak again. There was some new fellas this time, along with the others who heard me before. Five of the new ones prayed to receive Jesus as their Lord and Savior. One of them was a murderer (I found out later), but he held on to my hands and cried like a baby when he opened his heart to Jesus. Who am I to judge another man? Didn't the Lord have convicts on either side of Him when He was hung to death on that awful cross?

I'm also busy tellin' folks in town about Jesus. When you come back at Christmas, I want us to go over to Frank Austin's repair shop and talk to him more. I believe he's a good man, but he won't stop runnin' from the Lord. If I could only get him to take a little taste of God's goodness! Then he'd see for himself how sweet the Lord is! But when he sees me now, he likes to head the other way. Maybe he'll listen to you, though. After all, I listened to you when you talked to me that day in the diner and told me you loved me.

There are many more folks around here we need to have a talkin' to. They're not bad people, just misguided maybe, or closed-off might be another way to put it. Then there's the story of old man O'Brien. Lo and behold, he prayed with me yesterday to receive the Lord as his Savior! So did Charlie and Anne Katzenberg about a week ago. But Donna O'Brien has a stubborn heart. And we need to have a sit-down with Jeffrey Dimmitt, the banker. As you know, he does real well for himself financially. I think he might feel he has no need for God. But what amount of gold or silver will a man give in exchange for his very own soul?

Well, it's gettin' late here and my hand is hurtin' from all this writing. We'll miss you at Thanksgiving. But you make sure you come at Christmas. We got some ice fishin' to do.

Love, Dad

• • •

Two days later, I read Dad's letter to a group of between fifty and sixty people who had gathered for the memorial service. I sensed it was what Dad would have wanted. Most everyone mentioned by name in the letter was present, and their reactions varied according to what Dad had said about them. The purpose wasn't to embarrass anyone, but to share what were, in a sense, his last wishes.

Then I read from Paul's letter to Philemon. This had been Pastor Logan's idea, comparing Dad to Onesimus, who had formerly been a slave of Philemon. When Onesimus became a Christian and began to serve faithfully at Paul's side, Paul asked Philemon to grant Onesimus his freedom.

"I have sent him back to you in person," I read aloud from the letter to Philemon, "that you would have him back forever, no longer as a slave, but more than a slave, a beloved brother. . . . If then you regard me a partner, accept him as you would me. But if he has wronged you in any way or owes you anything, charge that to my account. I, Paul, am writing this with my own hand, I will repay it."

I looked at the family and friends. "'Charge it to my account,' wrote the apostle Paul. 'Let me pay the bill,' he said. Friends, that is what Jesus Christ offers each one of us without exception. He offers to take our sins upon Himself. That is what He offered my dad. And Dad accepted the offer. He allowed Jesus to do for him what he could never have done for himself. And you, Mr. Dimmitt? Are you going to let Jesus cover the price of your sins? There's not enough money in all the world to redeem your soul. Mrs. O'Brien? Mr. Austin? You heard what Dad said in his letter. You know he didn't write any of that to embarrass you.

He wrote that letter because he loved you. I speak to you with Dad's words, his cries for your souls. There are others in this room, too, that Dad didn't mention. You know who you are. Will you let Jesus redeem you from sin and death? Without Him, we're as limited as Onesimus was. But when we are set free in Christ, then real life begins."

• • •

Dad was laid to rest—just as he wished—at Riverside Cemetery next to Mom. I stayed at the farmhouse several days more, sorting through family papers and going over legal matters with my sisters, Shirley and June. (Mac couldn't get back from Africa in time to join us for Dad's memorial service.)

By the time everything was taken care of, it was only a few days before Thanksgiving. I decided to stay a while longer in Michigan, visiting with friends and family. Mr. Austin came to see me during this time. He looked as if he hadn't slept for several days. We talked briefly and he told me he wanted what Wilmot had. We prayed in the same room where Dad had given his life to Jesus Christ. The following day, a Saturday, I flew back to Los Angeles and got ready for school.

19

The Ocean Blue

WHEN I RETURNED to Talbot, I poured all my energies into my studies. I had a lot of catching up to do. One thing kept breaking my concentration. I couldn't stop thinking about my mother's fate. Maybe my emotions were raw because I had just stood at her grave site next to Dad's. She had been dead for almost five years, but I couldn't answer with certainty where she was spending eternity. I had just buried my father in the joyful expectation of being reunited with him in heaven one day. But what about my mom? *How can heaven truly be a happy place for me if she isn't there?*

I knew there was an afterlife; it was fundamental to my faith. Was Mom saved? Was her name written in the Lamb's Book of Life? To my knowledge, she hadn't made a decision to trust Christ for her salvation. Yet she was the one person I knew who had loved me unconditionally.

It didn't seem fair. *But what is fair in life?* As the writer pondered in the book of Ecclesiastes, "The race is not to the swift, nor the battle to the strong . . . but time and chance happen to them all."

Yes, the cold winter rains fit my mood.

When Christmas break arrived, it seemed everyone had left campus except me. The reality that I was an orphan, on my own and far from home, hit me hard. I needed to be strong and focused, using this perfect opportunity when things were quiet to prepare for midterm exams scheduled after New Year's. But just as sleep sometimes brings disturbing dreams more than needed rest, I couldn't surrender the doubts and fears I had concerning my mother.

I was walking and praying across the near-deserted campus one morning, *God, I have no idea how You'll answer this, but I have to ask You. Please let me know whether Mom was a believer or not. My heart is hurting so much; I long for peace.*

On an impulse, I drove to Manhattan Beach—twenty miles west. I parked the car and walked out the long concrete pier that extended far out into the ocean. I took a deep breath of the ocean air, tasting its saltiness. All I could hear was the thundering surf and the circling seagulls overhead. I noticed a group of surfers riding the waves. It looked like something I might like to try someday.

I walked farther out, passing an occasional fisherman. As I neared the end of the pier, I saw an older woman in a lawn chair, her fishing pole dangling over the metal railing. She was bundled up in a heavy blue coat, wearing sunglasses and an old floppy hat. "Catch anything yet?" I asked her.

"You betcha," she said, opening up the cooler beside her. "Got a few croakers here and a jack mackerel."

I nodded and kept walking toward the Roundhouse, an octagonal-shaped building with a greasy-spoon café and a bait-and-tackle shop where young teens liked to hang out. The roof of the Roundhouse was sagging, and the whole place looked like I felt.

At the end of the pier, I leaned on the railing and looked at the grayish-blue water below. The endlessly rolling waves had a calming effect. Suddenly I heard a woman's voice.

"I wouldn't do that if I were you."

I turned around and saw the old woman on the lawn chair glaring at me.

"What?"

"You're not thinkin' of jumpin', are you?"

"No, lady, not at all. Just thinking."

"From the looks of it, you've been thinkin' too much. Why don't you come over here awhile and keep me company?" She began rummaging about in her cooler. "Need a sandwich? I got an extra one here."

"Ah, that's okay," I said, walking over to her slowly.

"How about some coffee?"

"I'm fine. Really I am."

"How about some tea?" she said, smiling and holding up a tea bag.

"Well, if it won't be any trouble. Sure, I'll have a cup of tea."

Her face brightened and she removed her sunglasses. "No trouble at all, young man. My pleasure." She magically produced a thermos of hot water and some sugar packets. "Now where did I put my Styrofoam cups?" she muttered as she started rummaging in a large bag on the other side of her lawn chair. The surfers distracted me for a moment. As they maneuvered in and out of the barnacle-covered pilings, they seemed to defy death.

"You're not from around here, are you?" Her question got my attention again.

"No, ma'am, I'm not."

"Where you from?"

"Michigan."

"Michigan . . . that's a nice place. Here ya go." She handed me a steaming cup. "Be careful, it's hot. Goin' home for Christmas?"

I shook my head. "Actually, I just came back from home. I go to school in La Mirada."

"Really? You must go to Talbot, then."

"Talbot Seminary, yeah. You know it?"

"Sure I do, son. I'm a Christian. You picked a good school."

"I'm trying to get used to it," I said, feeling her eyes on me.

"So if I can be nosy, why aren't you goin' home for Christmas? You short of money?"

I laughed. "Well, I am now that I just made that trip, but no." I could see she was waiting for me to elaborate. "My dad just passed away."

"I'm sorry to hear that."

"At least he died knowing the Lord. I thank God for that."

"Amen," she said. "And your mom?"

"Mom died five years ago."

"Brothers? Sisters?"

"Yeah, but we're not close. It wasn't a very happy family, I have to say."

Just then, the woman got a bite on her line. She reeled for a minute or so, then shoved the pole into my hands. "Haul it in!" she shouted.

"Sure!" I said with a grin.

"You can have it if you catch it."

I laughed, not knowing where I'd keep or cook a fish. It was a fighter, but I reeled it in.

"Well done!" She clapped me on the back in excitement. "It's a sea bass! That's good eatin', son! Can you get the hook out for me too?"

I was glad to help. She dropped the fish in her cooler, and it flopped around for a few minutes. The woman handed me an anchovy to rebait the hook.

"I had a cousin who used to live in Michigan," she said. "A little town out there."

"Yeah? We have lots of little towns."

"Now, what was the name of it? She moved there a long time ago. Union City! That's it!"

I stared at her. "What did you say?"

"Union City. My cousin lived in Union City. Ever hear of it?"

"I was born there."

"Well, whaddaya know."

"What was your cousin's name?"

"Edith Joslin. She married a man named Wilmot McDowell."

"Ow!" I stuck myself with the hook. "Those are my parents!"

"Get outta town!" Her face lit up. "Why, you must be Jos!"

She grabbed me by the shoulders and took another look at me, sizing me up from head to toe. Her eyes were flecked with blue and gray, just like my mother's, just like the ocean around us.

"I never met you, but your mom told me about you. I'm Emma, your mom's cousin! Just call me Aunt Emma."

I was speechless.

"Can you believe it?! Last time I saw your mom was probably 1952."

My mouth felt like cotton, and I still couldn't get a word out.

"I'm Aunt Emma, son."

"Aunt Emma," I replied numbly.

"I grew up with your mom in Idaho."

"Idaho . . ."

"Don't bother baiting the hook, son. I'm going to take

you home for lunch. My two sons live nearby, and I want you to meet 'em. Help me pack up here."

I was still in shock. Finally, the words I had been struggling to say came out. "Aunt Emma, I need to ask you a question. Maybe you'll know the answer."

"Sure, son."

"Do you . . . by chance . . . happen to know if my mom ever trusted Christ as Savior and Lord?"

Emma set everything down. My anguish must have been obvious because I could see the deep compassion in her eyes. She realized how important the answer was going to be to me and took my hands in hers.

"Your mom and I were just teenagers when a tent revival come to town," she answered softly. "We went every night to the meetings. That was a big thing for us, you know, in those days. A lot of excitement." She squeezed my hands.

"And it was the fourth night . . . yes, the fourth night, as I recall, that she and I made our decision. We grabbed each other's hand and went forward to accept Christ."

"You did?"

"We most certainly did."

"Praise God!" I shouted, grabbing Aunt Emma and kissing her on both cheeks. "Aunt Emma, you are the answer to an impossible prayer!"

Several fishermen turned to see what the commotion was all about. "Praise God!" I shouted again. "Praise God from Whom all blessings flow!" I ran to the railing and shouted at the surfers. "Thank You, Jesus!"

I explained to Aunt Emma how only an hour and a half earlier I had prayed for God to let me know if my mom had been a believer, to let me know if I might meet her one day in heaven. Here I was in Southern California, not knowing a soul for miles—and certainly no one knew my mother. I never even expected an answer, but within ninety minutes God had let me know that my mother and father were not just buried together, but were in the Celestial City, worshiping with countless others around the throne of the Lamb. The tears were gone. There was no more pain.

Aunt Emma and I walked together to the parking lot, where I helped her pack up her car. I followed her home in my MG, met her sons, and enjoyed an excellent lunch. I had a family to be with at Christmas after all!

When it was time say good-bye, I took the scenic route back to Talbot, hugging the coastline as long as I could. I just wanted to be near the ocean. It stretched off in the distance as far as the eye could see, reminding me of eternity and the boundless grace of God. My life had been one scrape after another, one calamity after another, one crushing disappointment after another. But now I was experiencing incredible peace. A peace beyond understanding, the peace of God. I was ready to face the future, whatever it might bring.

Epilogue

I NEVER SAW my early dream of becoming a lawyer come true. Instead, I am still fulfilling the call to ministry that I answered more than fifty years ago when I joined Campus Crusade for Christ, the organization Bill Bright founded. As I travel thousands of miles a year (sometimes I think God should just give me wings to save some time) and speak to thousands of young people, I am in constant awe of what God has done in my life. My "job" never gets old; I never think of my responsibility to share the gospel of Jesus Christ as routine or something I have to do. I want to do this as long as God allows me. He has given me the strength and enthusiasm to live far beyond my limitations. For me, every day is exciting. Every time I clip on a microphone, I'm reminded of how good God is.

How could I have so many opportunities to speak about Christ? By God's grace, pure and simple.

For reasons I cannot begin to comprehend, God took everything that was stacked against me—my childhood trauma of sexual abuse, a home torn apart by alcoholism and anger, my struggles with feelings of inferiority that came out in stuttering speech—and made a brand-new Josh McDowell, a man born again by God's Spirit, a man undaunted by his past. My weaknesses showcase the power of His strength.

I am living proof of what Paul writes in 1 Corinthians 1:27-28: "God chose things the world considers foolish in order to shame those who think they are wise. And he chose things that are powerless to shame those who are powerful. God chose things despised by the world, things counted as nothing at all, and used them to bring to nothing what the world considers important" (NLT). Talk about describing me to a T!

With that empowerment I go on, boldly sharing the gospel with students on college campuses around the world. Some may think it foolish, but it's my life passion. "I am not ashamed of this Good News about Christ. It is the power of God at work, saving everyone who believes" (Romans 1:16, NLT). No matter how smart someone may be, no matter how radical a person's views, no matter how privileged or poor, the gospel can transform people's lives.

God transformed my life and He will transform yours, if you let Him. Don't let the circumstances that seem to hinder you keep you from embracing Jesus Christ as Lord of your life. He loves you passionately and fervently desires a relationship with you. Jesus says, "Look, I am making everything new! . . . To all who are thirsty I will give freely from the springs of the water of life" (Revelation 21:5-6, NLT). He stands at the door of your heart and knocks. Will you open the door of your heart and invite Him in to take over every aspect of your life? Will you receive Him as Lord and Savior? You can do it right now, honestly praying a simple prayer:

> Lord Jesus, I need You. I know I'm a sinner. Thank You for dying on the cross for my sins. I repent of my sins. Forgive me and cleanse me. I believe You are the only way, truth, and life. I trust You as Savior and Lord right now. Come into my life and change me. Thank You that I can trust You. In Christ's name I pray, amen.

Once you've received Jesus as your Savior and Lord, He wants you to grow, and I do too. I want to help you see Christ truly change your life from the inside out. Go to www.josh.org/undaunted, where I will be able to share with you many things to help you grow in your new faith and solidify this wonderful new direction in your life. God bless you, now and always.

Acknowledgments

Our thanks go to the Tyndale Momentum team at Tyndale House Publishers—Jan Long Harris, Sarah Atkinson, Sharon Leavitt, and Nancy Clausen for their key roles in making this project happen; to Bonne Steffen, indefatigable and talented editor, who always pushes for excellence, assisted by Annette Hayward and her team who checked and rechecked the manuscript; to research assistant Matt Kinne, who had an ever-positive attitude and offered tireless support; to Ron and Martin Chard, two brothers who grew up in Union City during the 1940s and '50s and were able to provide important historical details; to several of Josh's boyhood and college-age friends—Charles Wilson, David Aviza, and Dick Purnell—who knew him well and contributed their recollections to this story; to our wives, Dottie McDowell and Cheryl Krusen, for their love and prayers; to Cristóbal's father, Bill Krusen, who passed away a few weeks after this book was completed: "The apple does not fall far from the tree."

Discussion Guide

1. Why, as a kid, did Josh think there was no hope or love anywhere in the world? Have you ever felt the way he did when he said good-bye to God as a twelve-year-old?

2. Mr. Turner, Faith's dad, asked Josh, "What is your relationship with Jesus Christ?" Why was this a confusing question to Josh at the time? How did he answer it? What would your answer be to that same question?

3. When Josh's friend Tim died, Josh wondered why the good perish and the wicked thrive. Have you ever wondered this? What conclusion have you come to?

4. What happened to suddenly change Josh's military plans? Have you ever had circumstances line up perfectly to help you change directions in life?

5. How did the Christian group at Kellogg Community College handle their interactions with Josh? Have you ever interacted with unbelievers like they did? If so, how were you like the Kellogg group? How were you different?

6. Who was Alan Cobb, and what role did he play in Josh's story? Do you have someone like Alan in your life?

7. What is the legal-historical method of proving something? How do you think it compares to scientific evidence?

8. How was Josh's perception of God as heavenly Father affected by his earthly father? How has your own perspective of God (good or bad) been influenced by your father?

9. Why did Josh go to Europe? What did he hope to accomplish, and why did he come home thinking he had failed? Did he fail?

10. Josh felt like Pastor Logan's sermons were sometimes preached directly at him. Have you ever felt this way? What messages have you heard recently that really spoke to you?

11. When did Josh truly know that Christianity was real? Have you had a similar moment of certainty in your life?

12. What role did forgiveness play in Josh's story? How has it played a part in your own life?

13. What circumstance brought Josh home after being away at Wheaton College? How was this detour an amazing part of God's plan for him?

14. What did Pastor Logan have to say about relationships and the Cross? What did this mean for Josh? How do you see this truth affecting your life?

15. Josh identified with the child in the Bible who offered a few fish and loaves of bread to Jesus in order to feed the multitudes. What did Josh have to offer God? How did God multiply those gifts? What do you have to offer?

16. How did "a cemetery become a seminary" for Josh? Has God ever drastically changed your view on something? Explain.

17. Why is the word *undaunted* an apt description of Josh? What does it mean to you?

18. What are the main themes of Josh's story that stand out to you? How do you relate to his testimony?

Notes

xi *"People are born for trouble"*: Job 5:7, NLT

2 *"Will You Still Love Me Tomorrow?"*: Gerry Goffin and Carole King, a song originally recorded by the Shirelles in 1960.

2 *"A city that is set on a hill"*: Matthew 5:14, NKJV

77 *"The Bible says that if anyone is in Christ"*: See 2 Corinthians 5:17.

80 *"My Lord and my God!"*: See John 20:28.

111 *I am trying here to prevent anyone saying*: C. S. Lewis, *Mere Christianity* (New York: HarperCollins, 2001), 52.

115 *"There may be, and, as the writer thinks"*: Frank Morison, *Who Moved the Stone?* (Grand Rapids, MI: Zondervan, 1987), 193.

116 *"The conversion and apostleship of Saint Paul"*: Quoted in Hannah More, *An Essay on the Character and Practical Writings of Saint Paul*, Volume 2 (London: T. Cadell and W. Davies, 1815), 286–287.

116 *I have been used for many years*: Quoted in John Phillips, *Exploring 1 Corinthians: An Expository Commentary* (Grand Rapids, MI: Kregel, 2002), 343.

117 *"It was impossible that the apostles"*: Simon Greenleaf, *An Examination of the Testimony of the Four Evangelists by the Rules of Evidence Administered in the Courts of Justice* (Grand Rapids, MI: Baker, 1965), 29.

134 *"God has chosen the foolish things"*: See 1 Corinthians 1:27.

140 *"When they came to the place"*: Luke 23:33-34, NASB

142 *I had the steady, full peace*: See Philippians 4:7.

145 *"the common enemies of man"*: See http://www.jfklibrary.org/JFK/Life-of-John-F-Kennedy.aspx?p=4.

159 *"Verily, verily, I say unto you"*: John 5:24

160 *"Come unto me, all ye that labour"*: Matthew 11:28

172 *"I am crucified with Christ"*: Galatians 2:20

180 *"The heart is deceitful above all things"*: Jeremiah 17:9

180 *'Take up your cross daily'*: Luke 9:23

181 *"Search me, O God"*: Psalm 139:23

181 *"See if there be any wicked way"*: Psalm 139:24
192 *'Here am I, Lord'*: See Isaiah 6:8.
194 *I was remembering the story in the Bible*: See Mark 6:1-13.
197 *"Love, joy, peace"*: See Galatians 5:22-23.
216 *When I was a child*: See 1 Corinthians 13:11.
217 *Now we see dimly in a mirror*: See 1 Corinthians 13:12.
217 *And now remain these three*: See 1 Corinthians 13:13.
235 *"I have sent him back to you in person"*: Philemon 1:12, 15-19, NASB
238 *"The race is not to the swift"*: Ecclesiastes 9:11, NKJV

About the Authors

Josh McDowell has given more than 24,000 talks to over 10 million young people in 118 countries since beginning his ministry in 1961. He is the author or coauthor of 112 books, selling over 51 million copies worldwide, including *More Than a Carpenter* (more than 15 million copies in print worldwide), which has been translated into more than 85 languages, and *The New Evidence That Demands a Verdict*, recognized by *World* magazine as one of the twentieth century's top 40 books.

Josh continues to travel throughout the United States and countries around the world, helping young people and adults bolster their faith and scriptural beliefs. Josh will tell you that his family does not come before his ministry—his family *is* his ministry. He and his wife, Dottie, have four children and eight grandchildren.

Cristóbal Krusen is founder and president of Messenger Films, headquartered in Tampa, Florida. He is an honors graduate of NYU's School of Film and Television and holds an MFA from the Broadcast Cinema Department of Art Center College of Design. Among his feature film credits as a writer/director are *Final Solution*, *More Than Dreams*, *First Landing*, *The Bill Collector*, and the Spanish-language films *¿Con Quién Te Vas?* and *Ropa Nueva para Felipe*. His most recent film, *Undaunted*, tells the early life story of Josh McDowell. Cristóbal is the author of *Let Me Have My Son* and *My Journey . . . from Skepticism to Faith*.

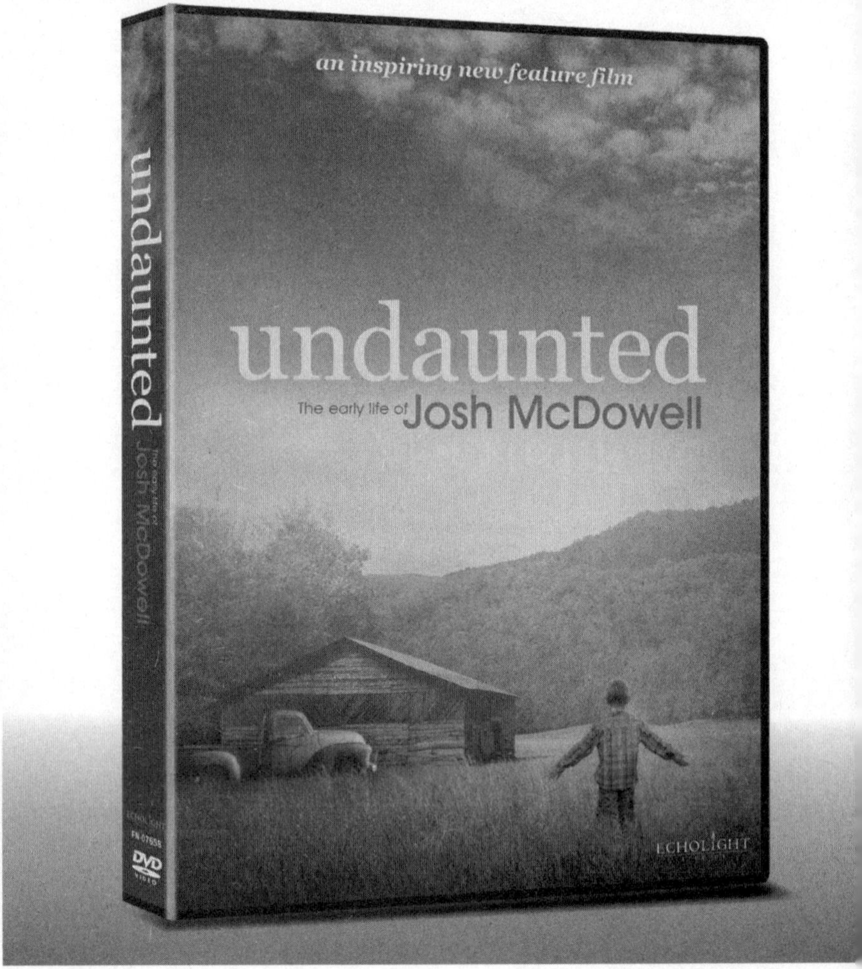

Watch Josh McDowell's story come to life on screen!

www.undauntedmovie.com